FIRST STEPS
NeoWhimsies

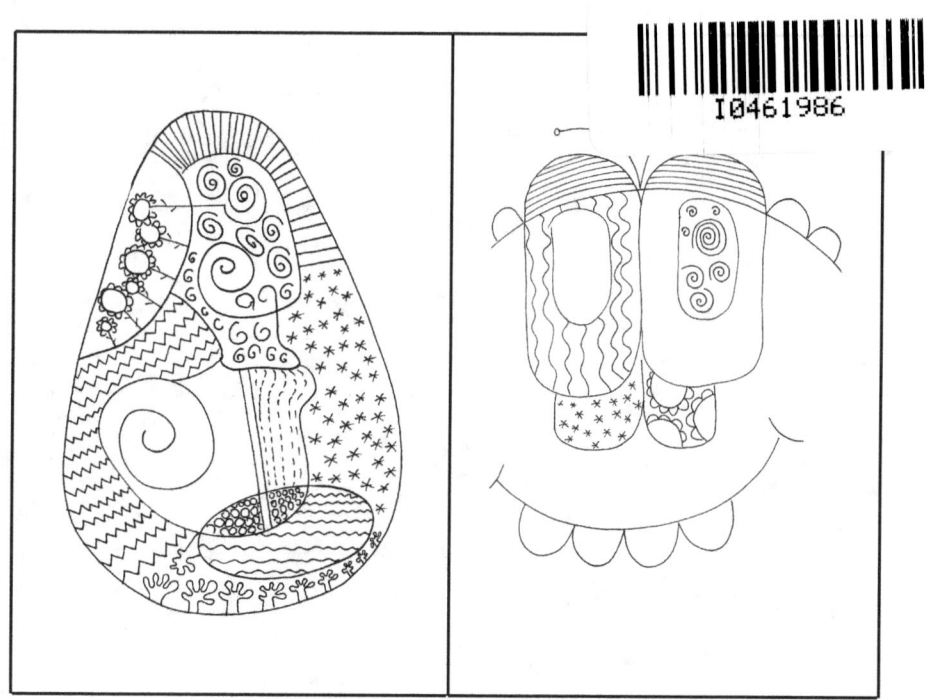

NEOPOPREAISM

ink drawing
FOR BEGINNERS

ILLUSTRATED by SERGE E. MIKHAILOV
NeoPopRealism PRESS

2

A book "FIRST STEPS: NeoWhimsies: NeoPopRealism for Beginners" by NeoPopRealism PRESS with illustrations by Serge E. Mikhailov invites the readers on an enlightening journey teaching how to open yourself to imaginative and whimsical world of the ink drawing. Albert Einstein said, "Imagination is more important than knowledge. For knowledge is limited, whereas imagination embraces the entire world, stimulating progress, giving birth to evolution. It is, strictly speaking, a real factor in scientific research."

The common use of the term 'Imagination' in arts is for the process of drawing new images that have not been previously experienced with the help of what has been seen before or at least only partially or in different combinations.

An illustrator of this book, Serge E. Mikhailov confessed that for him imagination is equal to memory and that he can "imagine" only things that he saw in the real life. Unfortunately, majority of people have the lack of imagination. However, this book is a try to teach the readers how to unlock their imagination and discover new dimension in arts. We hope it will be your step forward as it was a first step for Serge E. Mikhailov.

FIRST STEPS
NeoWhimsies

NeoPopRealism
ink drawing
for BEGINNERS

ILUSTRATED by Serge E. Mikhailov
NeoPopRealism PRESS

First published in 2012 by NeoPopRealism PRESS
PO BOX 366
New York, NY 10013

NeopoprealismPress@mail.com

"FIRST STEPS: NeoWhimsies: NeoPopRealism Ink Drawing for Beginners" by NeoPopRealism PRESS
Illustrations by Serge E. Mikhailov

Published in the United States of America
Language: English

ISBN-13: 978-0615641553
ISBN-10: 0615641555

12 13 14 15 16   10 9 8 7 6 5 4 3 2 1

This book teaches how to draw NeoWhimsies - the NeoPopRealism ink images for beginners.

www.neopoprealism.org

CONTENT

INTRODUCTION

NeoPopRealism art style and ink drawing concept was created by artist Nadia Russ in 1989.

It was an experiment. She was trying to connect to the Universe and let the Universe use her as a conductor when she created her drawings. She didn't want to follow any other artists' achievements, she decided to create absolutely new art form, like Picasso (Cubism), Dali (Surrealism), Andy Warhol (Pop Art) and a few other worldwide known artists had done.

Nadia Russ took her ink pen and began to draw a flowing line, which turned into shapes, figures, often faces. Then, some sections (or all), which appeared, she filled with the repetitive patterns. She never uses eraser because if a mistake made, it disappears with the following repetitive patterns that balance the whole composition. Her work was unique, no one did anything like this before.

Later, January 4, 2003, Nadia Russ created a word NeoPopRealism and internationally announced new style of visual arts. Today, her artwork can be found in the private, corporate and museums' art collections worldwide. She lives in the U.S.

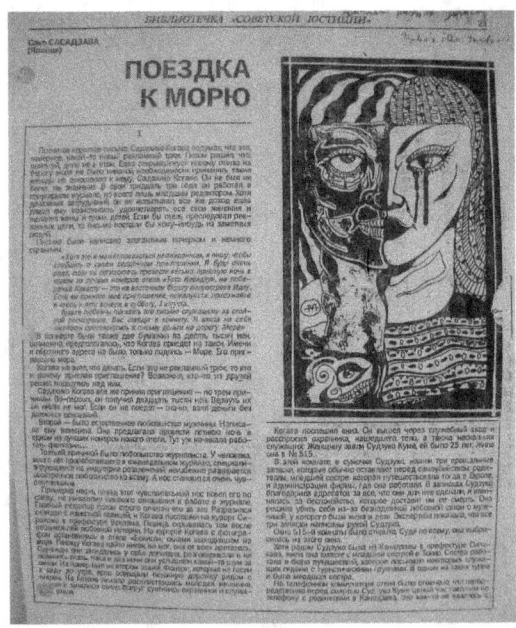

Nadia Russ illustrated a story by Saho Sasadzava for the *Russian Justice* Journal, 1992, Moscow, Russia

Get Inspired

hen you focus on your success, you fall into the trap of comparing yourself to other people, feeling envious. Instead, focus on getting better every day. Focus on excellence. Use your strengths for a bigger purpose beyond yourself. Focus on what you are giving instead of what you are getting, it makes every your step more rewarding and meaningful.

Get the black ink pen *Foray Rolle Rollerball Medium 0.7 mm* or *Sharpie* and a piece of cardstock paper 8.5"x11". Cut it into two pieces - 5.5"x8.5" each. Now, you need one piece.

You would like to create something very unique and that's not always easy to do. You need to learn how to connect to the Universe and open your mind to the higher powers.

Close your eyes for a moment. Imaging that your consciousness leaves your body and fly to the Space where there are no people but only super speed and super powers. Forget about your daily life experiences. No noise should disturb you except, possible, music. You are not you any more; you are a part of the Universe.

Slowly open your eyes. Try not to look around, look only at your piece of the plain white paper. This is the beginning. . . Now draw.

If you after all couldn't draw the NeoPopRealism image, go to the next pages of this book. After you learn how to draw with the all offered tips and tricks, come back to this page again and let see what will happen.

This book will teach you how to draw NeoWhimsies. NeoWhimsies are the simple NeoPopRealism ink drawings. This book is filled with NeoWhimsies! Learn how to draw NeoWhimsies and you will be able to create more complicated, NeoPopRealism artwork and exhibit it in the art galleries.

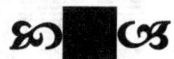

Draw the Eggs

The following pages will show you how to create step-by-step   the NeoWhimsies eggs. NeoWhimsy is a simplified NeoPopReaism ink drawing, made out of combination of sections filled with the imaginative repetitive patterns. Each drawing - NeoWhimsy - has different character, it made using different patterns. The following visual instructions will teach you how to create the drawings; they will lead you from the beginning to end of the drawing process. Every following image includes new detail(s). The final NeoWhimsies look like this:

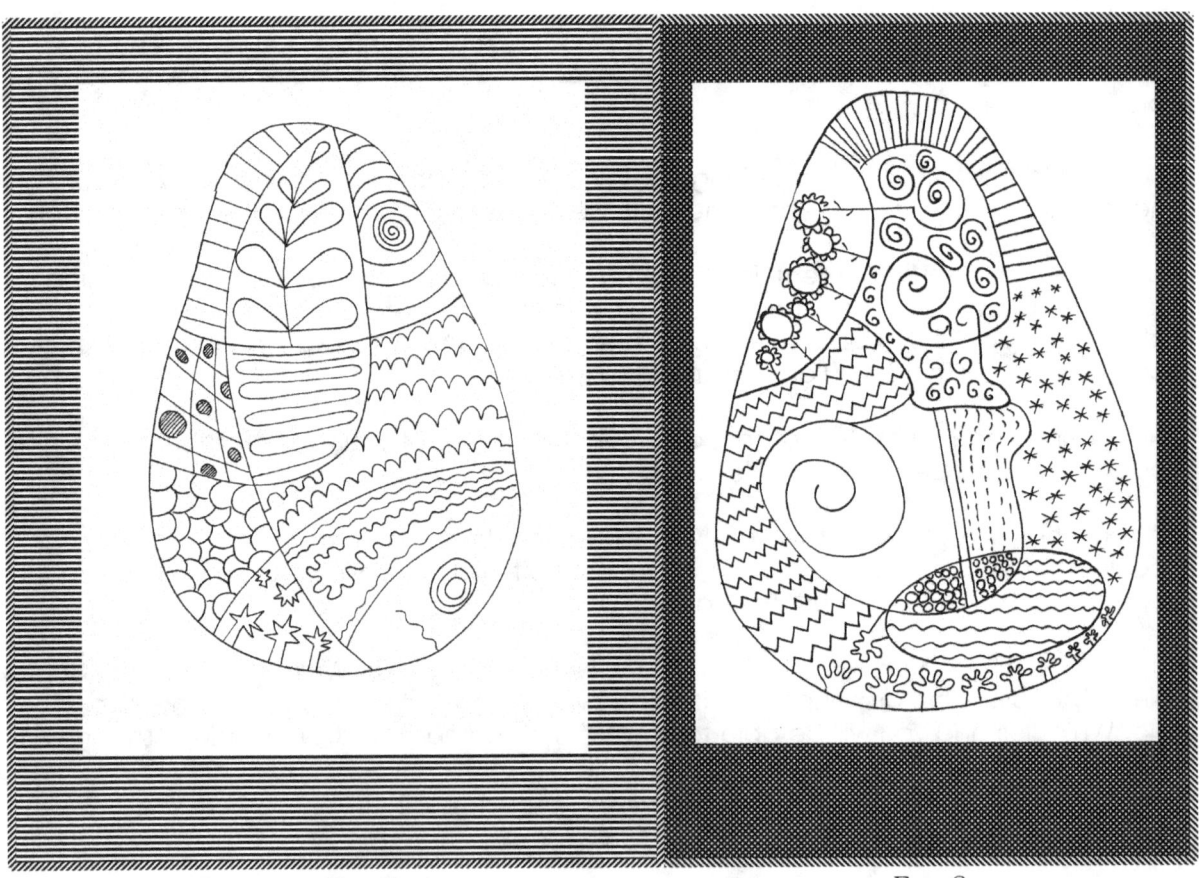

Egg 1   Egg 2

How to Draw Egg 1

Before you start to draw NeoWhimsy *Egg 1,* learn how to draw the repetitive patterns used in this drawing. You will find them below.

Egg 1	**Horizontal strips** / **Breeze up-side-down**	**Squares with small dark circle**
Whirle	**Leaves**	**Snake**
Connected waves	**Hands**	**Caviar**

Next pages will teach you step-by-step how to draw NeoWhimsy Egg 1. You will learn how to draw the flowing line - a contour , how to divide an image into the spaces, and then how to make your egg look whimsical and artistic. You will learn how to fill the spaces with different repetitive patterns. When you create your NeoWhimsies you develop your artistic skills.

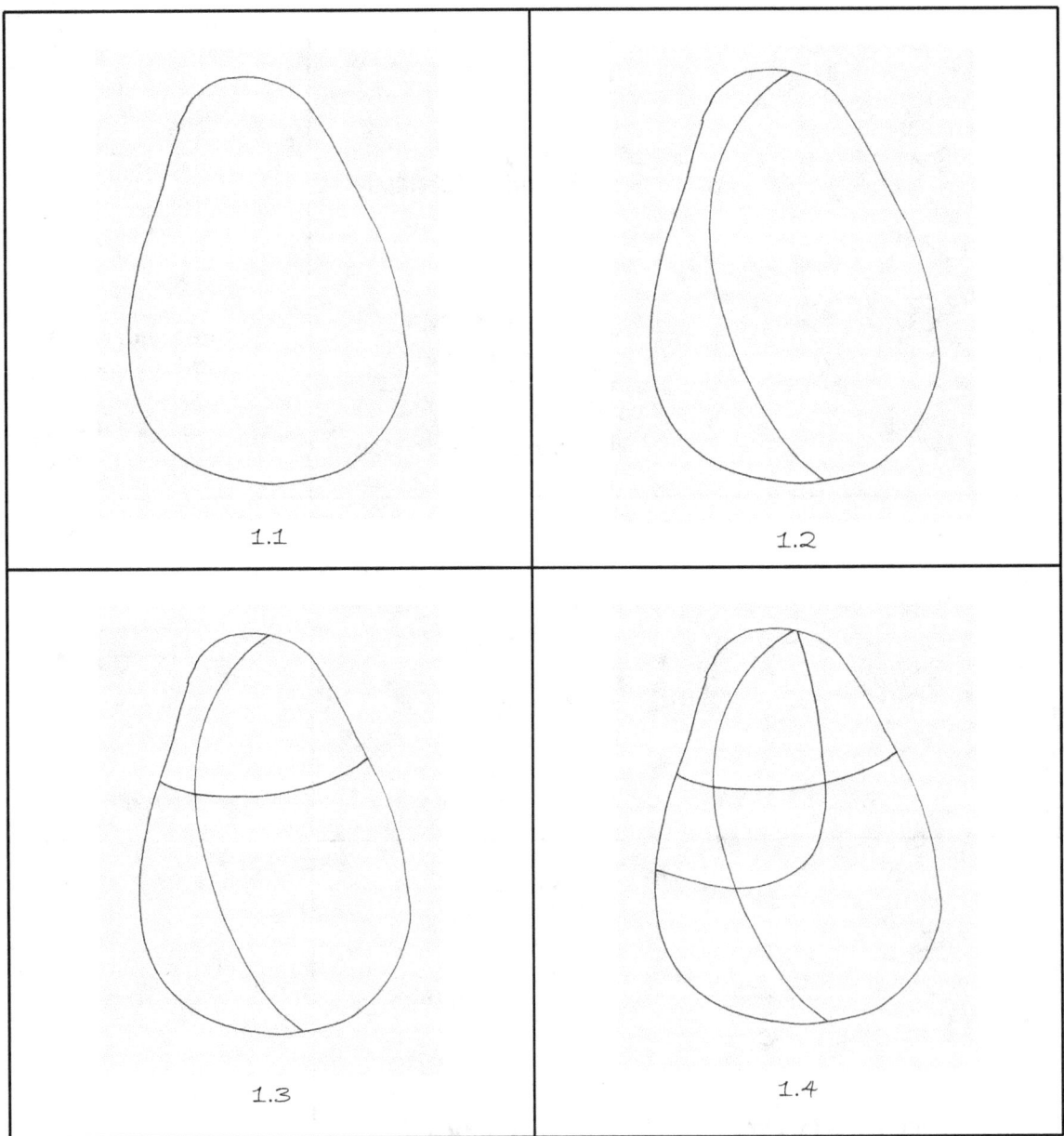

1.1

1.2

1.3

1.4

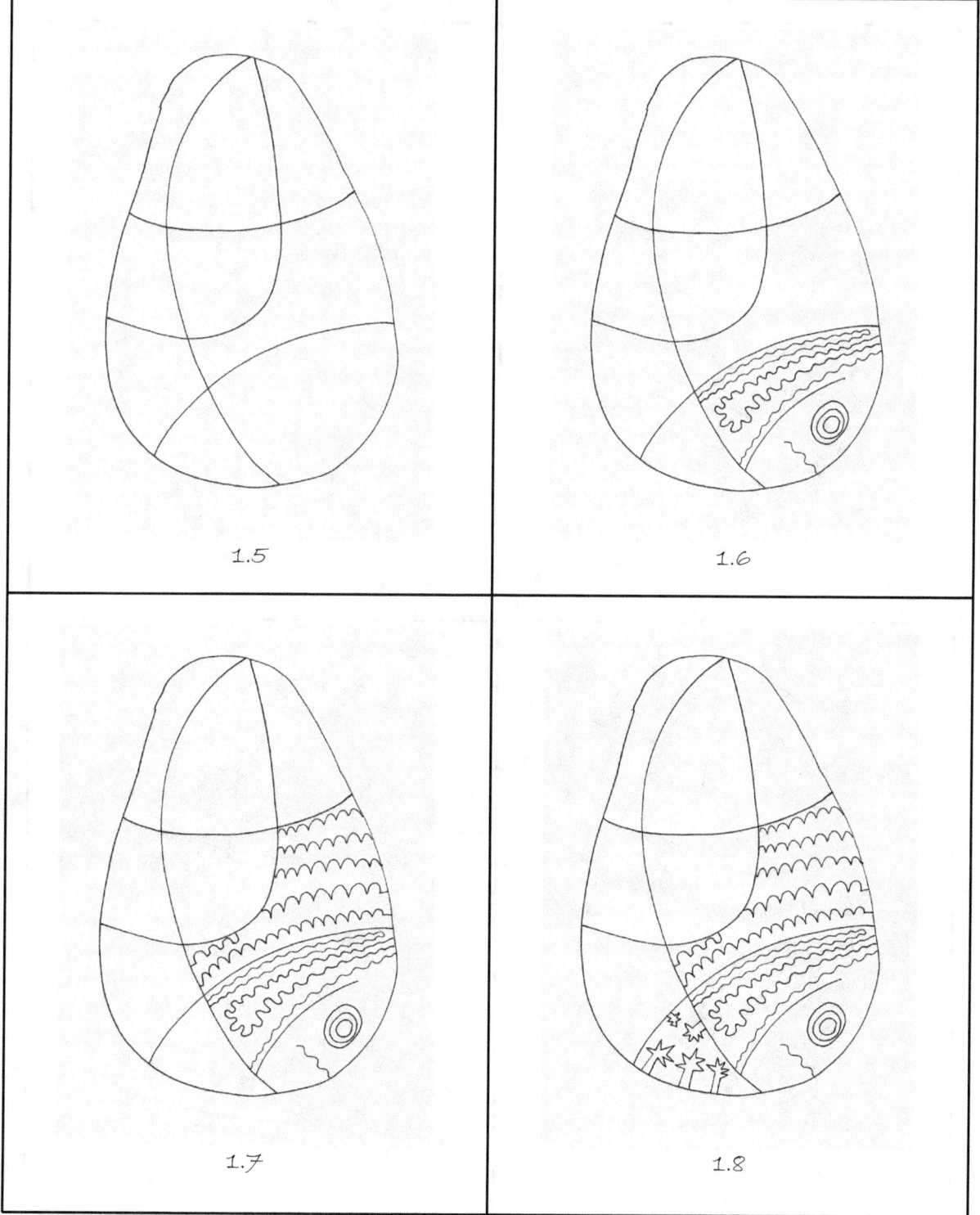

1.5

1.6

1.7

1.8

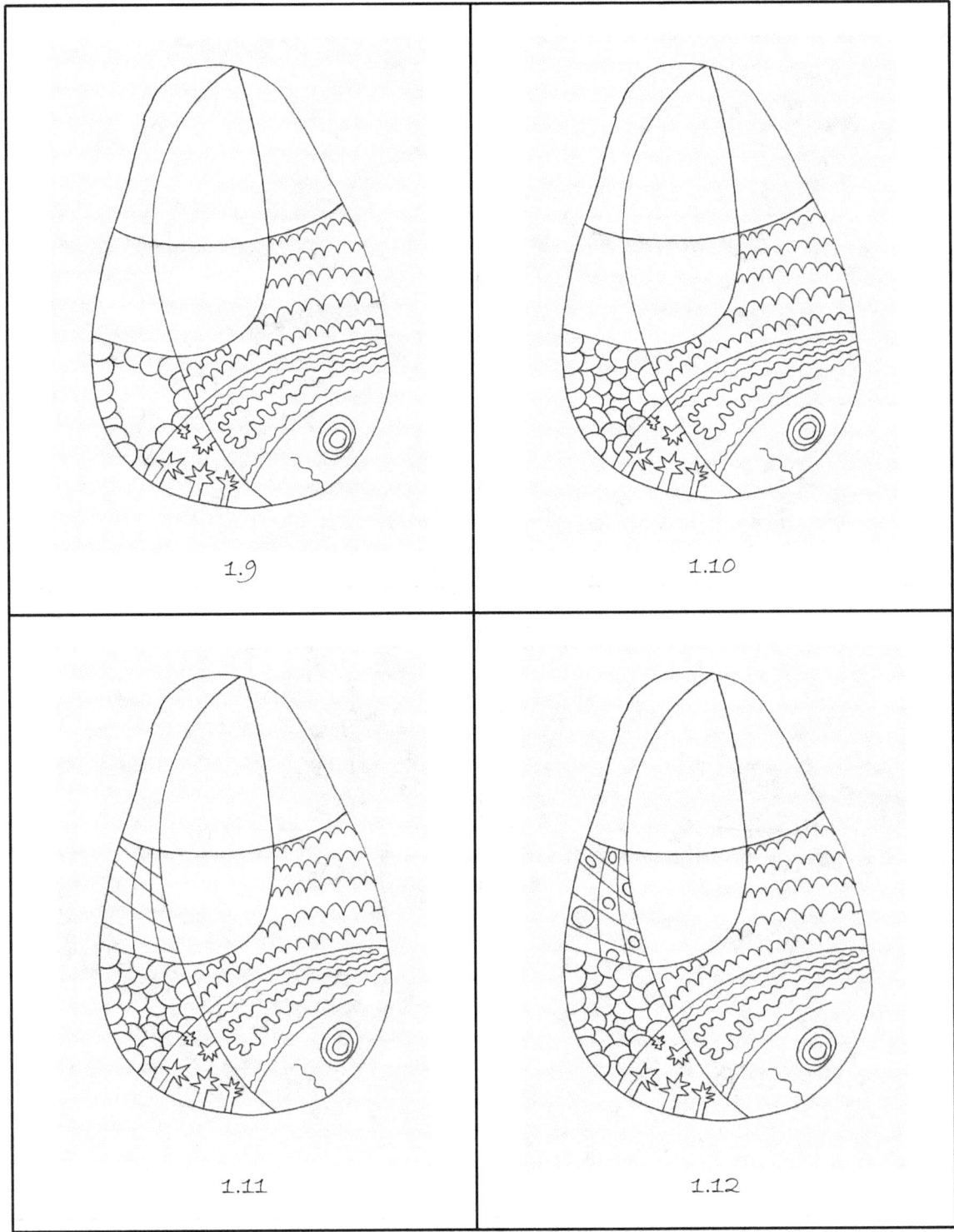

1.9

1.10

1.11

1.12

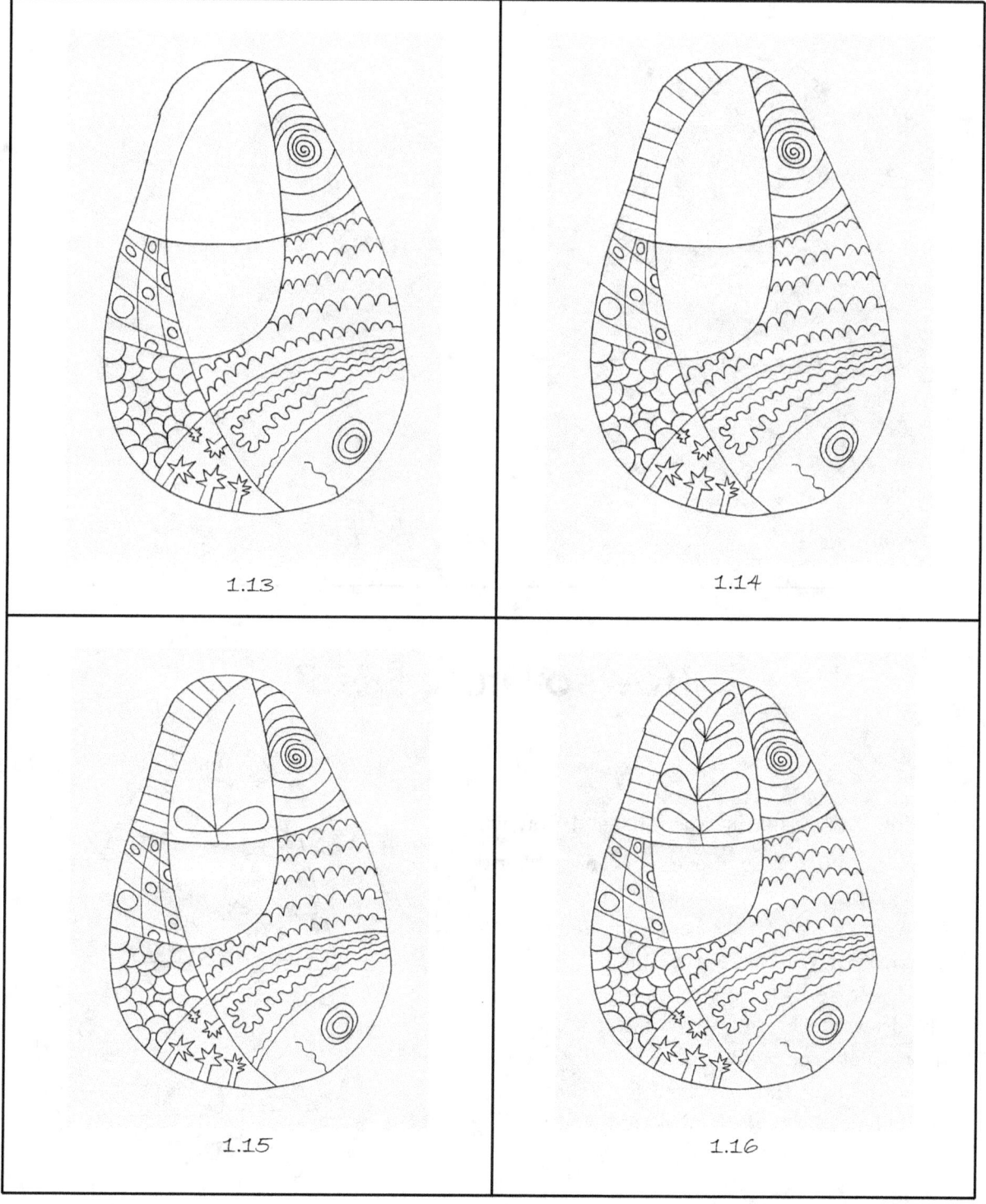

1.13

1.14

1.15

1.16

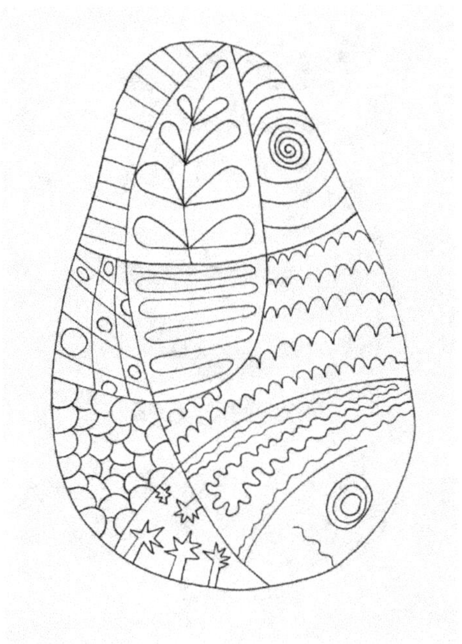

1.17

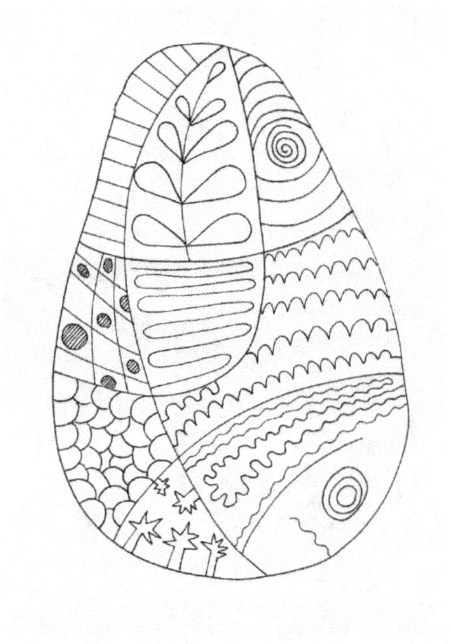

1.18

How to Draw Egg 2

Follow the visual instructions and you will learn how to create the exuberant artworks like Egg2. Serge, when he created NeoWhimsy Egg 2, used his imagination. Do not worry if you make a mistake. You do not have to erase it. It visually "disappears" when you draw more repetitive patterns because these patterns will balance the entire composition of the drawing. The composition and balance are very important and can be achieved through the training.

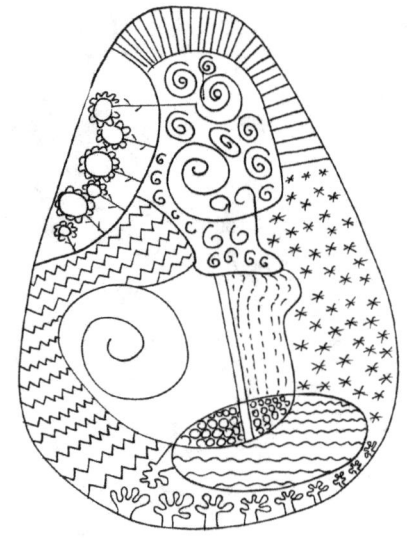

The Egg 2

Before you start to draw NeoWhimsy The Egg 2, learn how to draw the repetitive patterns, used in this drawing.

Vertical strips	Whirles / Waves	Face
Sun flowers	Zig–Zags	Stars
Dots	Snakes	

Follow the visual Instructions and you will be able to create the beautiful images of eggs.

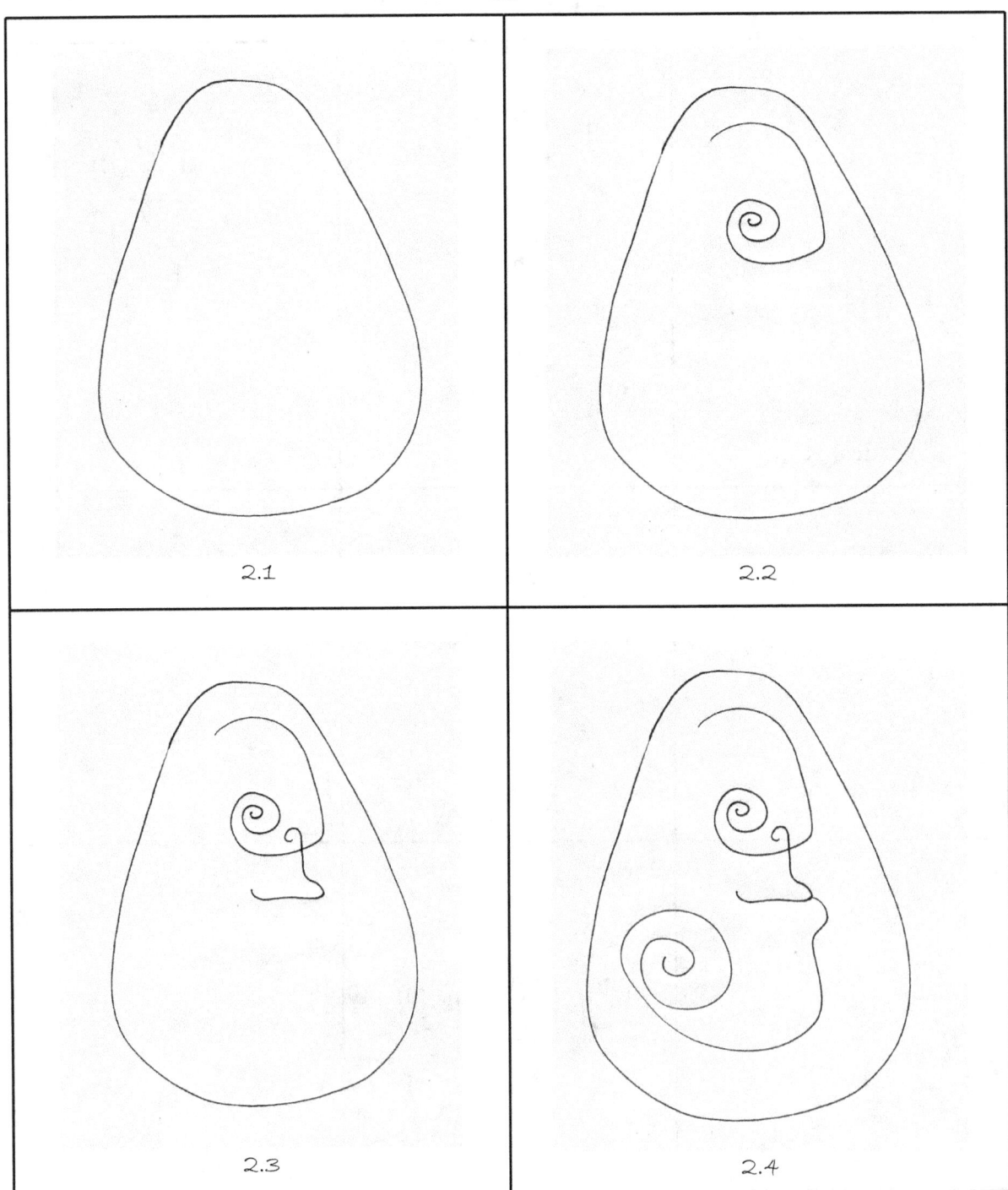

2.1

2.2

2.3

2.4

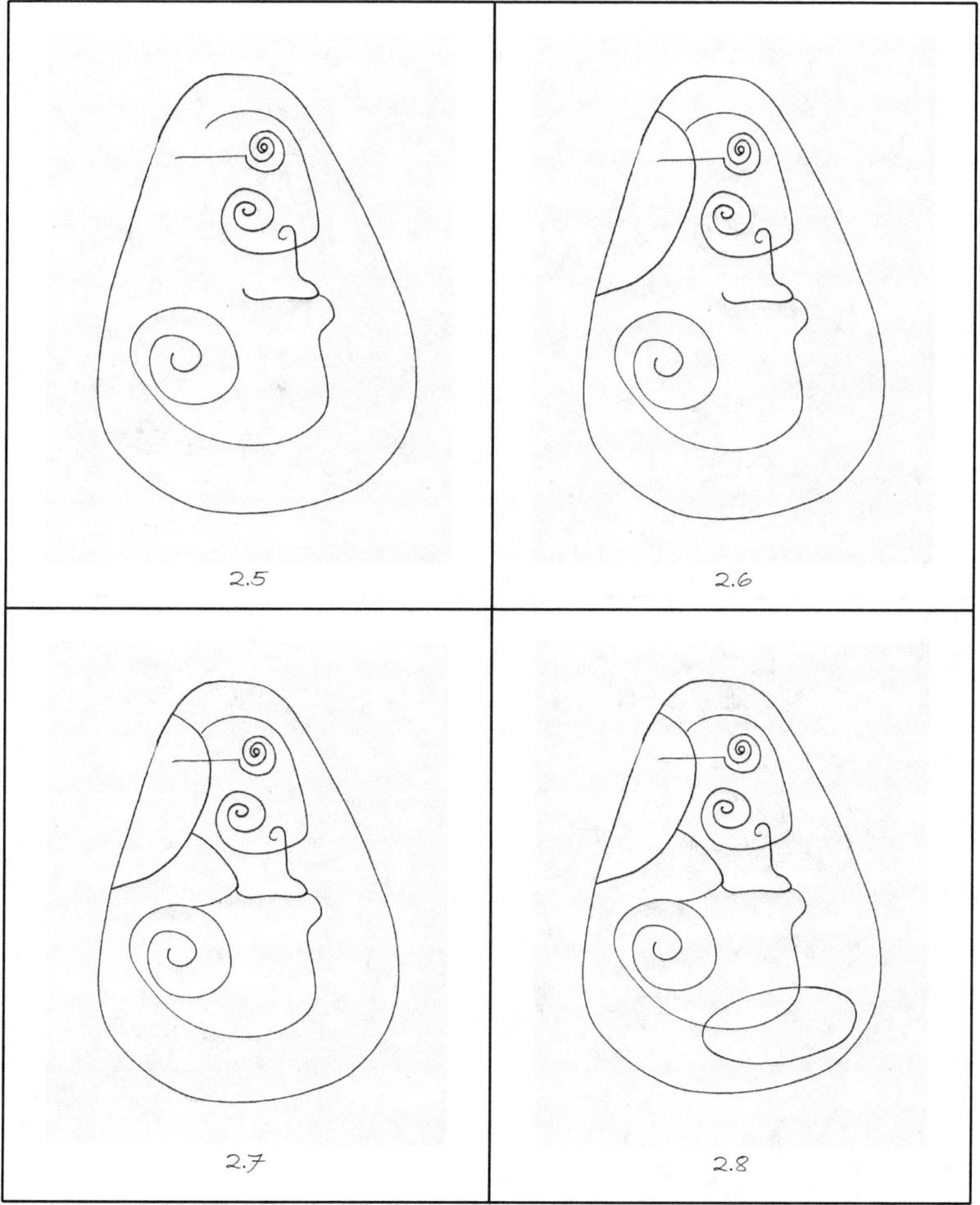

2.5

2.6

2.7

2.8

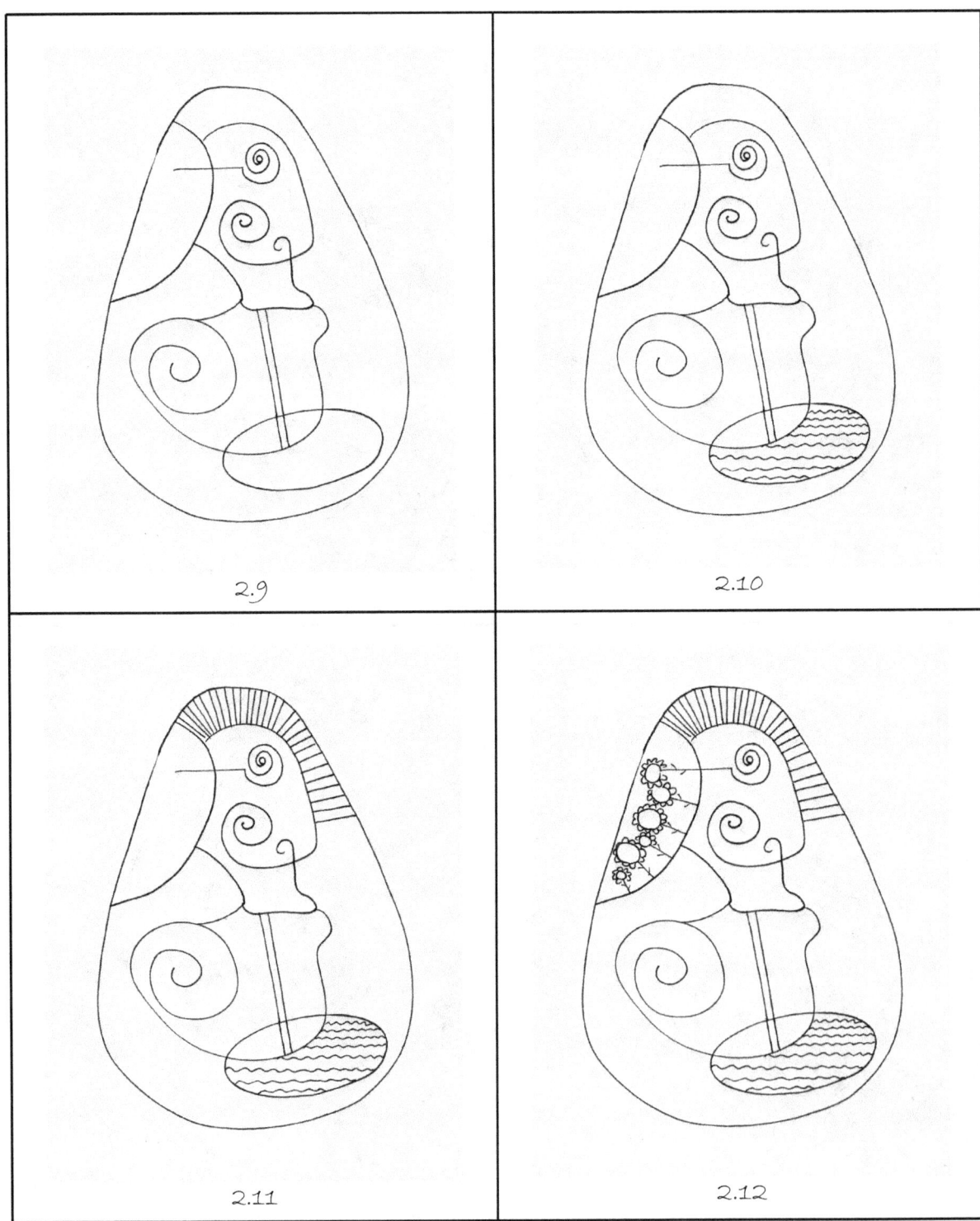

2.9

2.10

2.11

2.12

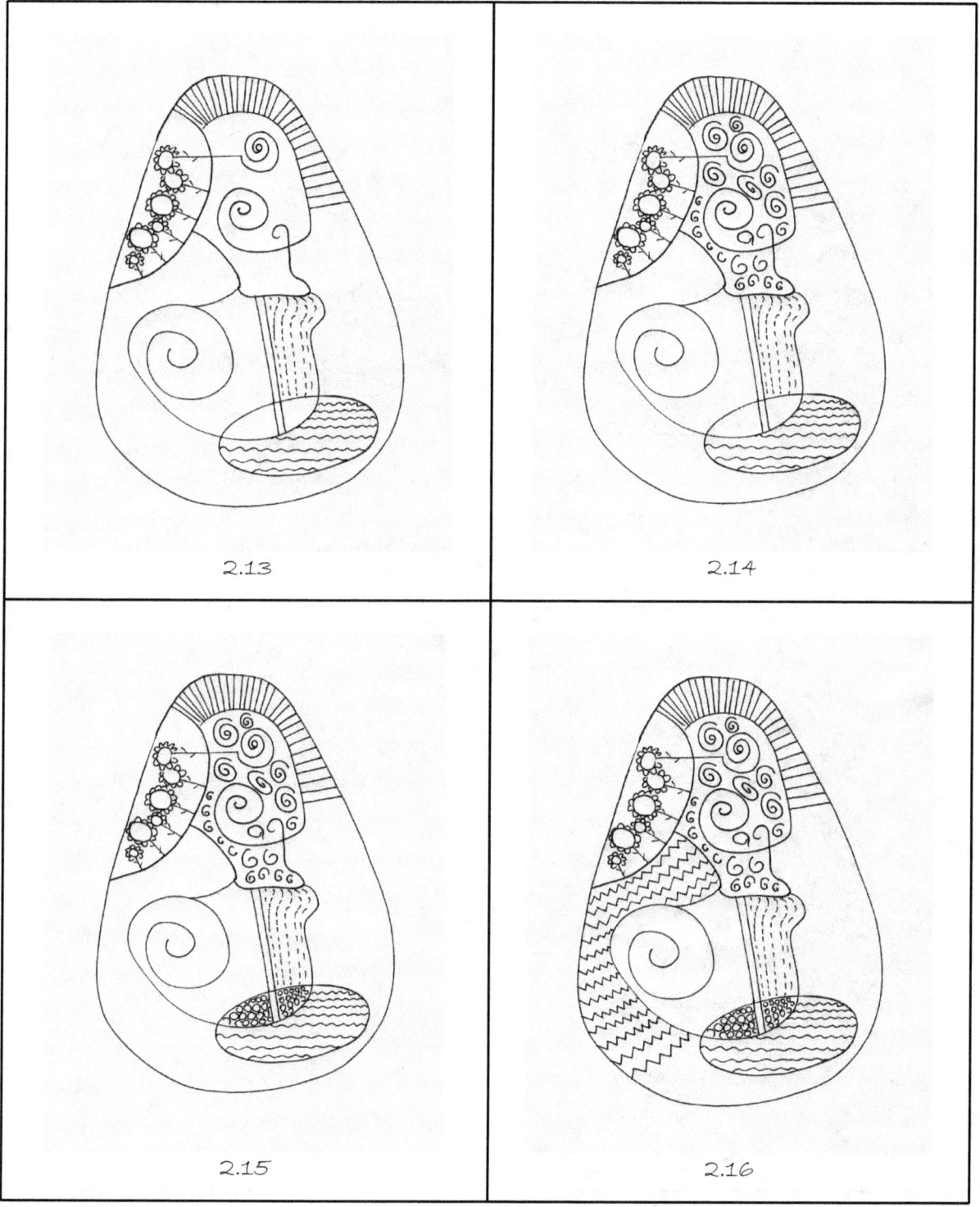

2.13

2.14

2.15

2.16

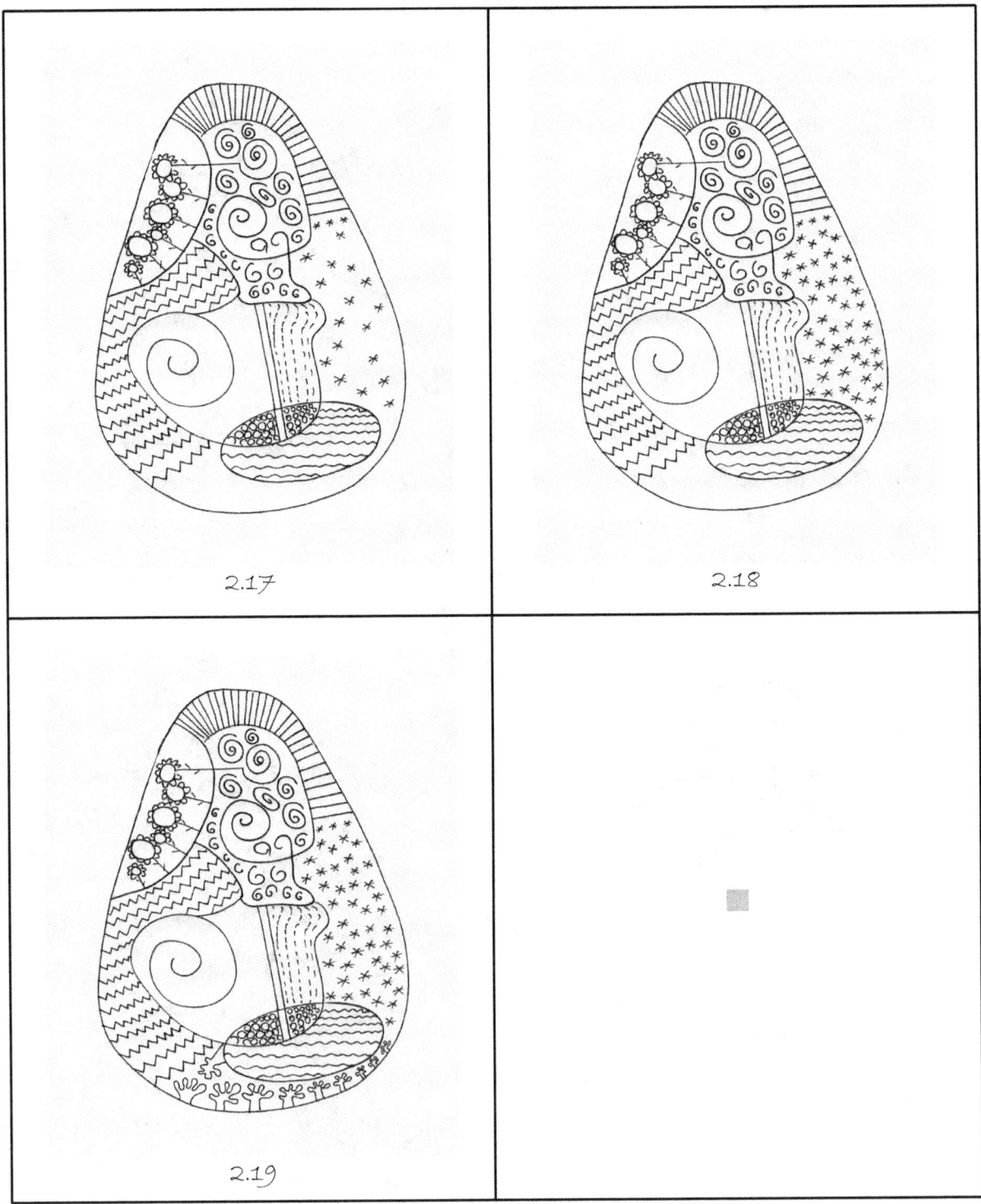

2.17

2.18

2.19

Draw the Eggs with Serge
Here and Now

*U*se next pages for your training. Get your ink pen and fill sections of the eggs with different repetitive patterns. Employ your imagination, create the patterns following your creative instinct or use those you know. Some section(s) leave blank. The repetitive patterns' (ornaments) drawing is very rewarding. When you draw you enter the meditative state of mind. There is a deep connection between meditation, health, and happiness. The drawing helps you to experience calm and peace of mind, increasing your energy and vitality. More you practice, better you feel and better your artistic skills will be. Imagination is a very important artistic quality. Imagination is considered a power of the mind, a creative faculty of the mind, and the mind itself when in use. It is a process of the mind used for thinking, creating, fantasizing, more. More you practice, better your imagination.

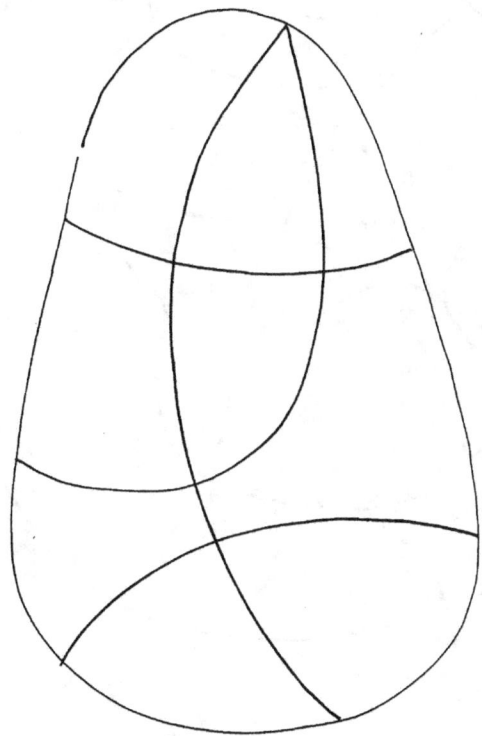

The Egg 1

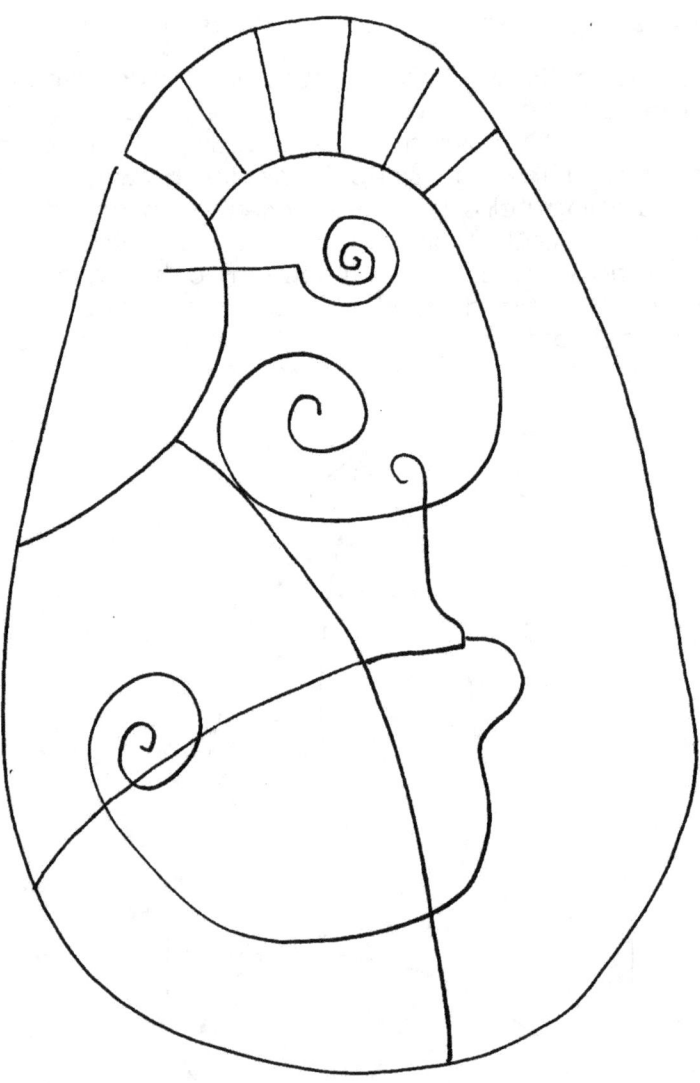

The Egg 2

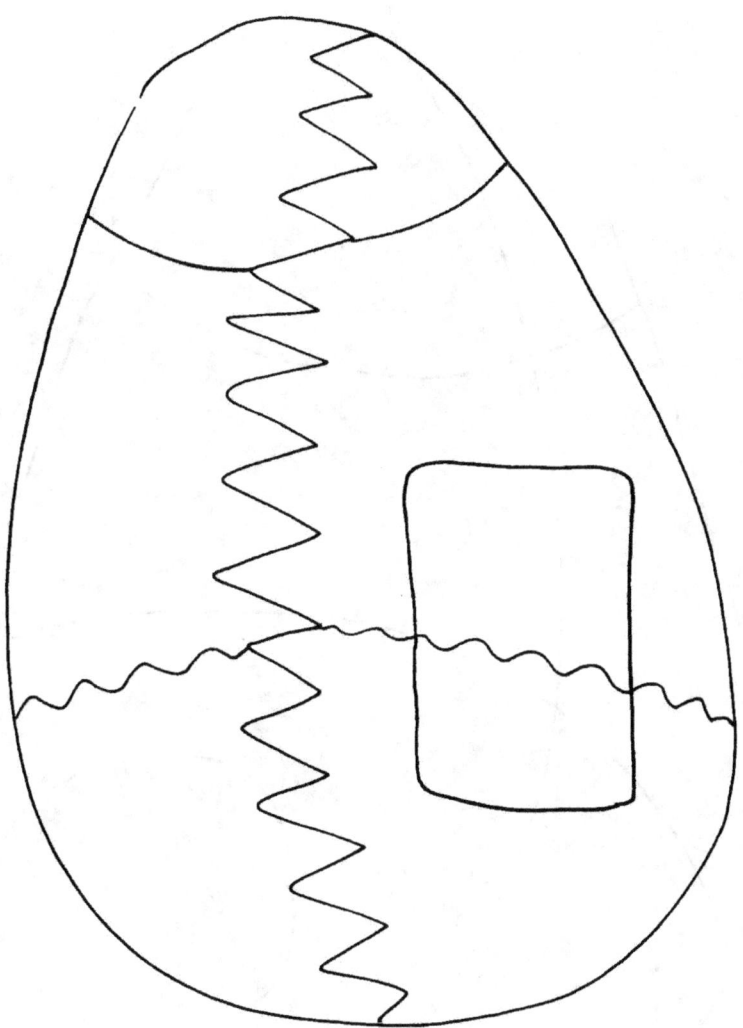

The Egg 3

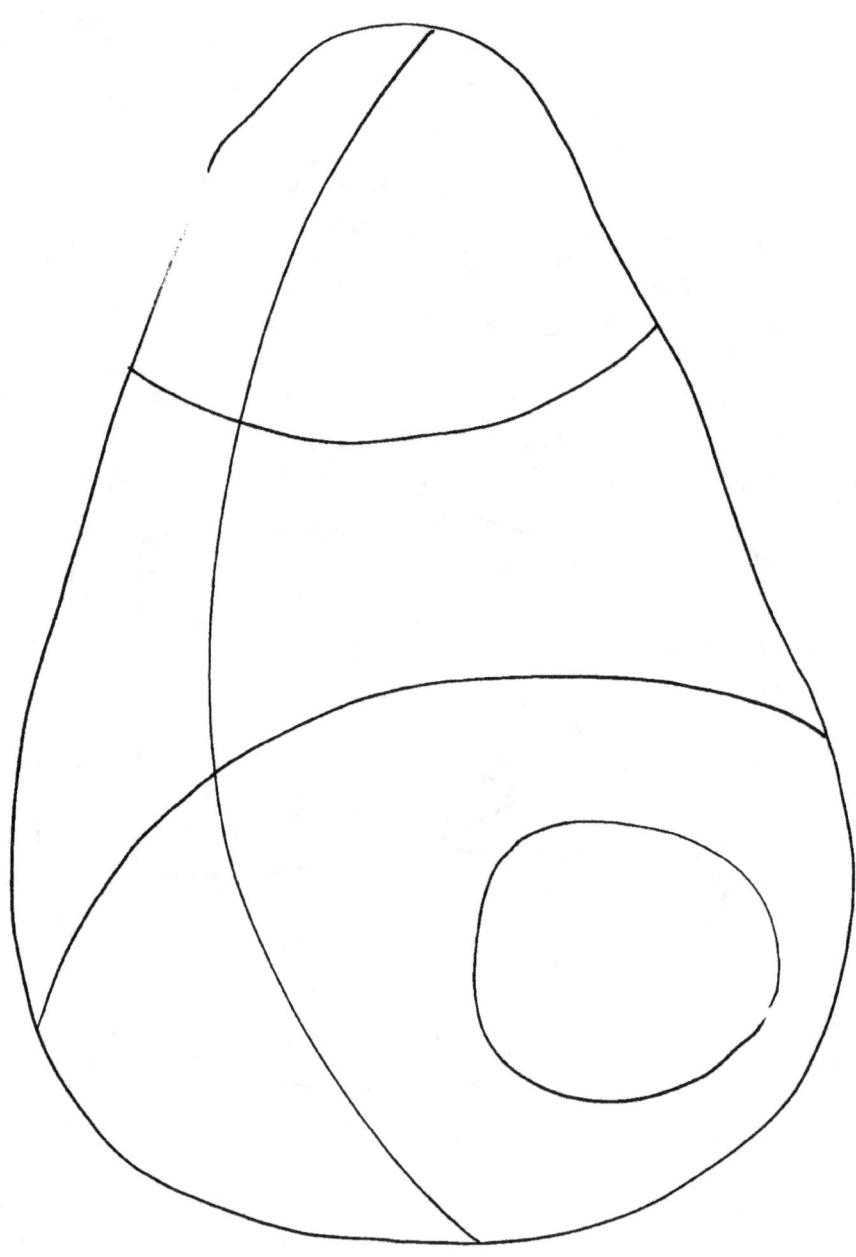

The Egg 4

Draw the *Butterflies*

The following pages will show you how to create step-by-step the Butterflies.

These NeoWhimsies made out of combination of sections, which are filled with the different repetitive patterns. Each butterfly's drawing has different character and made using different or similar patterns. The visual instructions will lead you through the drawing process from the beginning to end. Every following image includes new detail(s). The final images look like this:

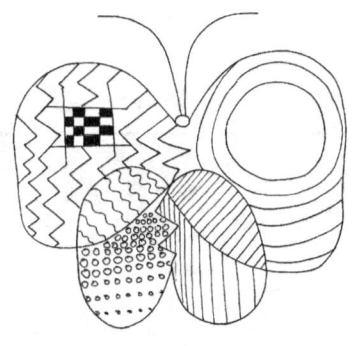

The Butterfly 1

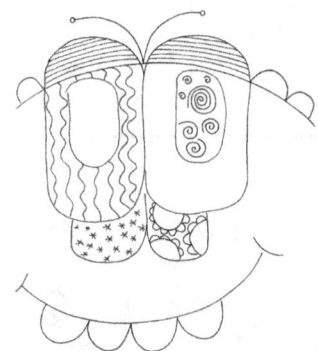

The Butterfly 2

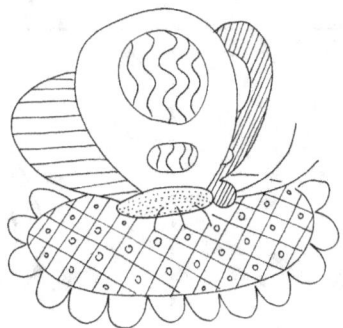

The Butterfly 3

How to Draw Butterfly 1

This page includes the patterns. Before you start to draw NeoWhimsy Butterfly 1, learn how to draw the repetitive patterns used in this drawing.

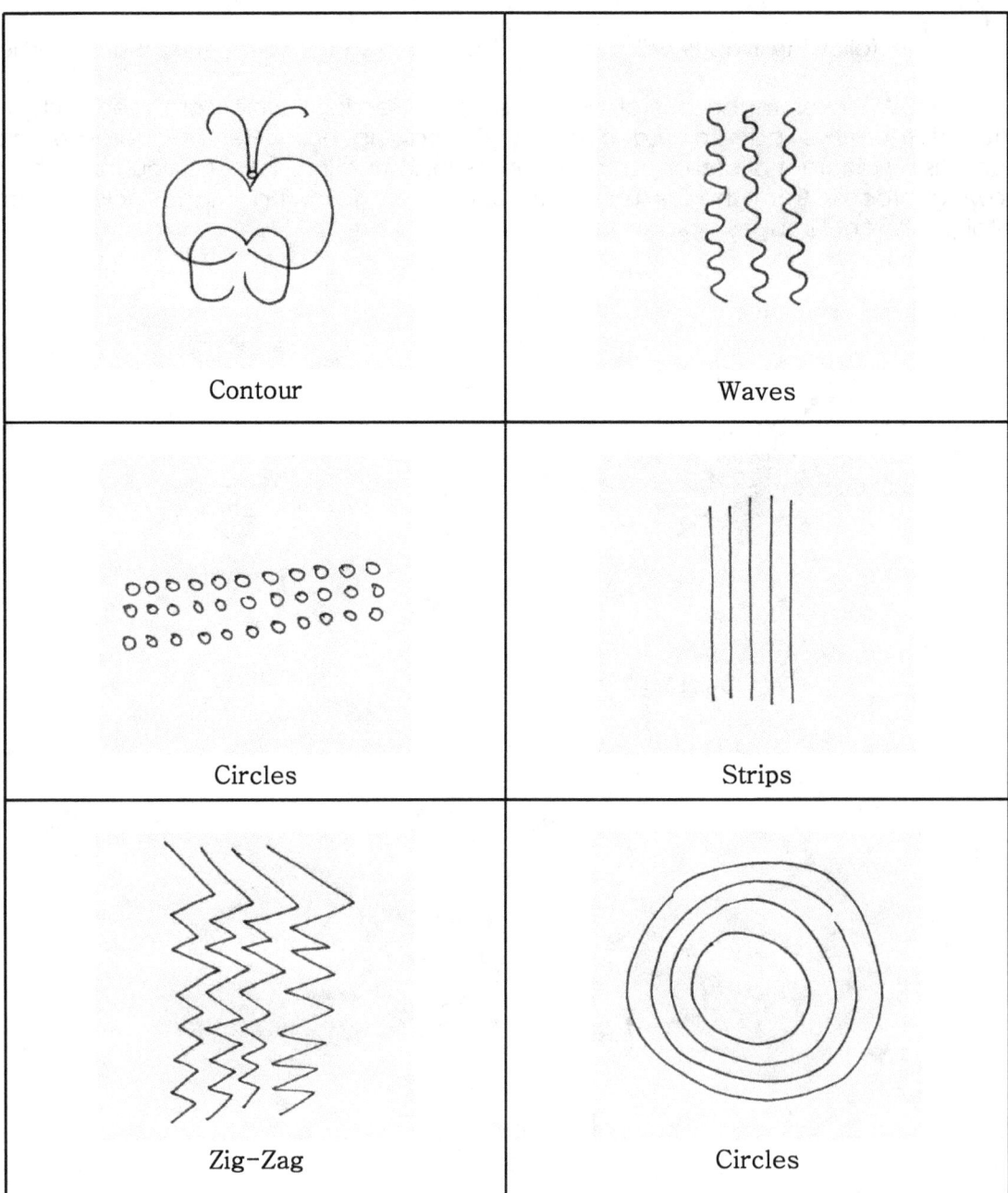

Contour	Waves
Circles	Strips
Zig-Zag	Circles

These pages show step by step how to create NeoWhimsy Butterfly 1. Follow the visual instructions. Easy flowing line creates the sections, which later will be filled with different repetitive patterns. When you'll understand the process of the image developing, you will be able to create the images on your own. Free your mind, get creative!

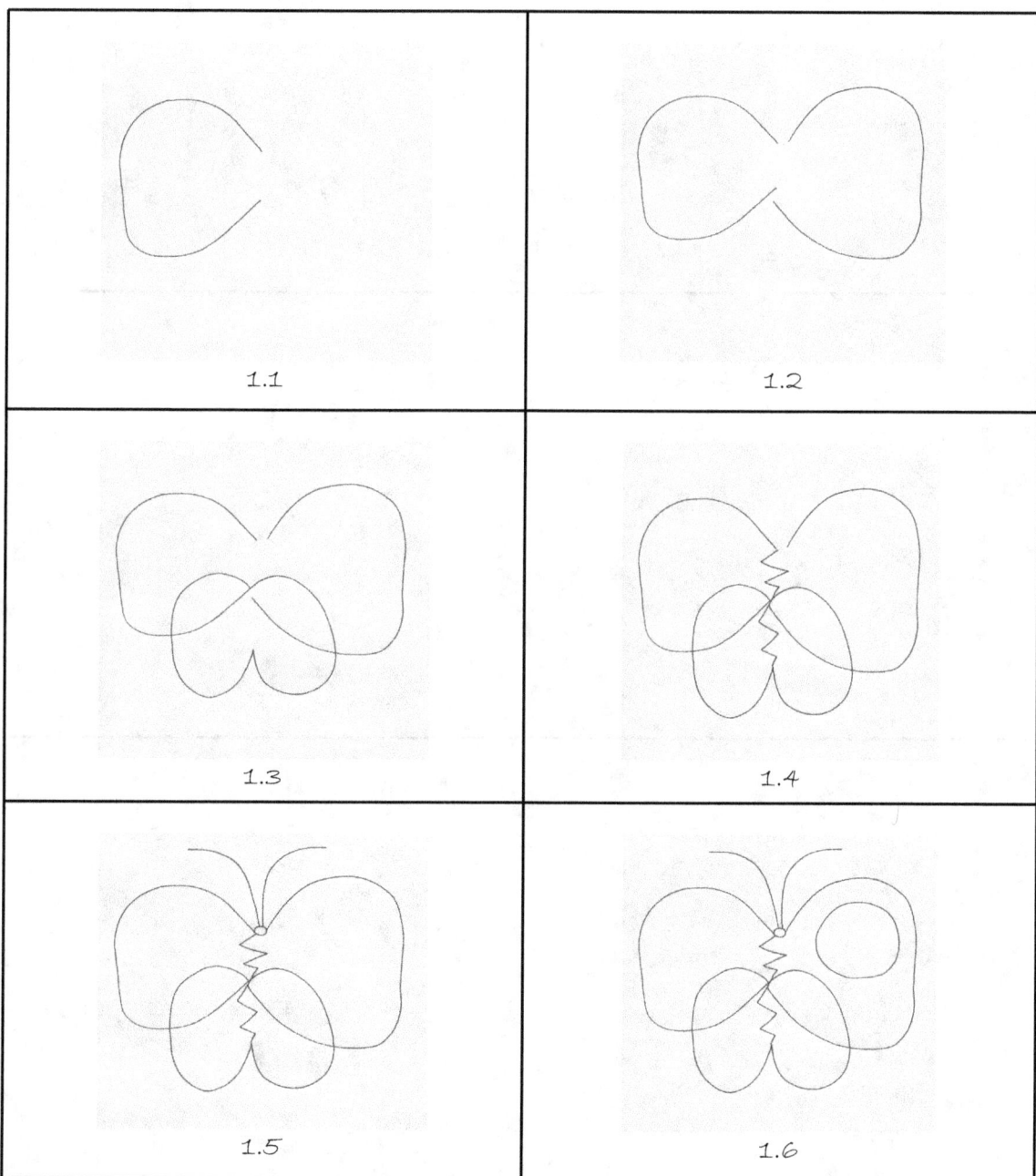

1.1

1.2

1.3

1.4

1.5

1.6

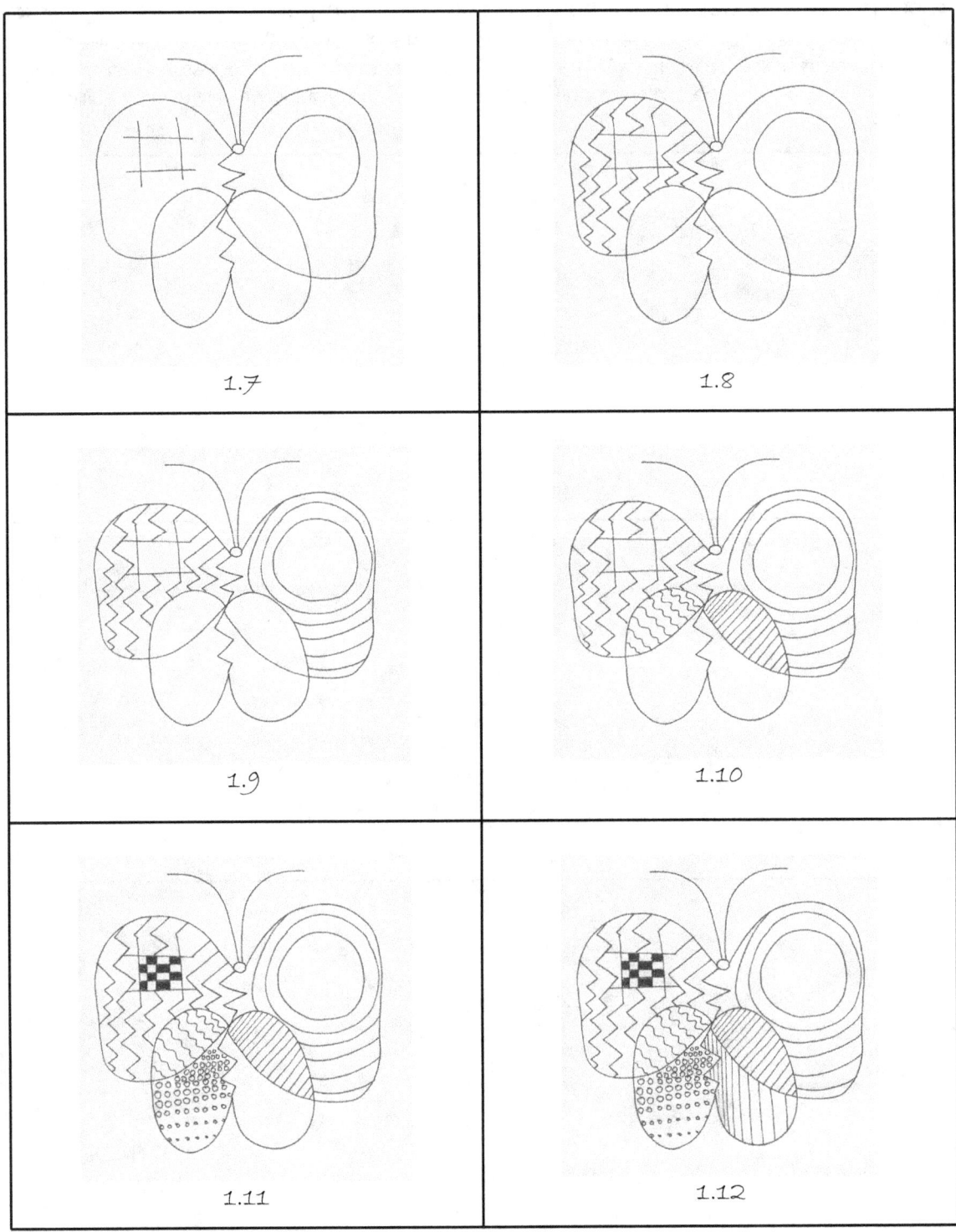

1.7

1.8

1.9

1.10

1.11

1.12

The NeoWhimsies look beautiful when they are framed. Frame your drawings and display them.

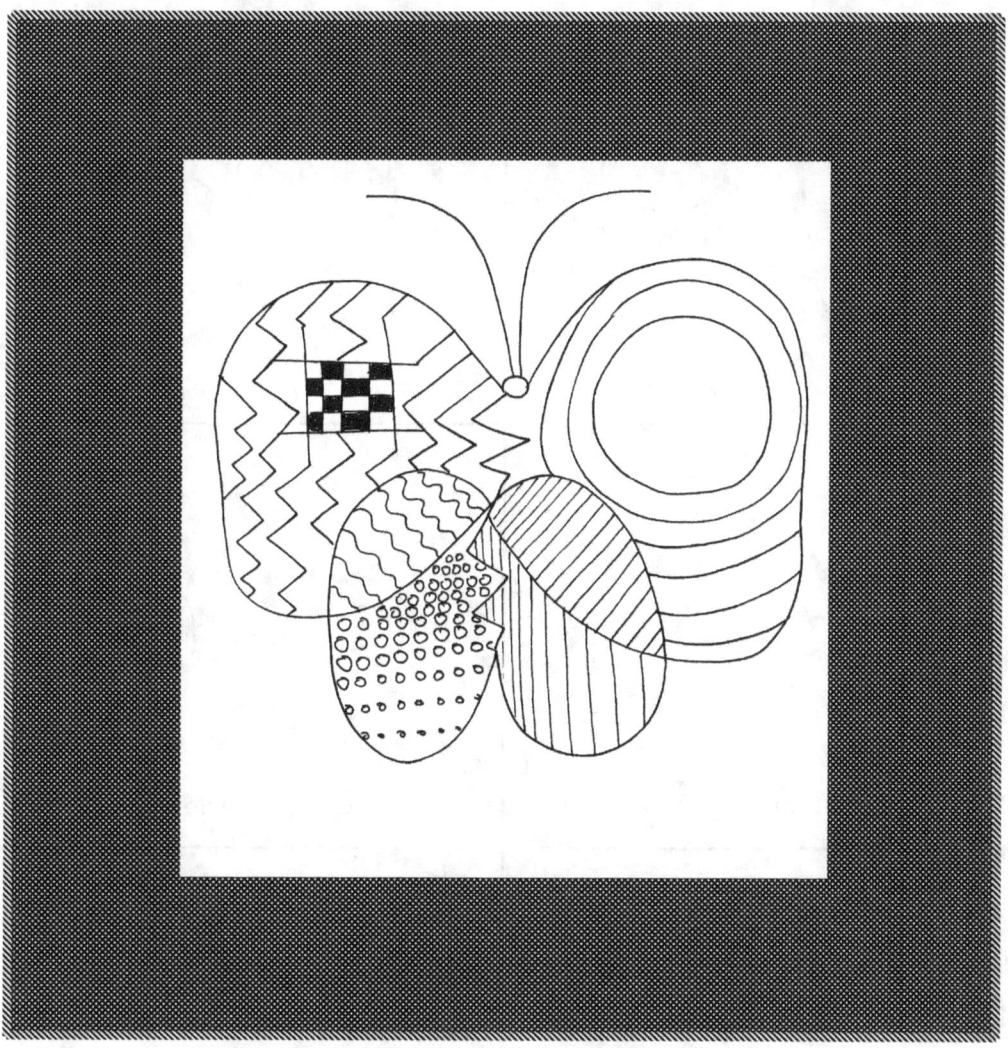

Serge E. Mikhailov, *The Butterfly 1*

How to Draw Butterfly 2

This page includes the repetitive patterns' samples. Serge used these patterns when he drew NeoWhimsy Butterfly 2.

Contour of Butterfly 2	Sun flowers
Stars	Whirles
Strips	Playful face

Next pages show you step by step how Serge created NeoWhimsy Butterfly 2. Follow the visual instructions. When you'll understand the process, your imagination will lead your hand freely and you will be able to create different NeoWhimsies on your own.

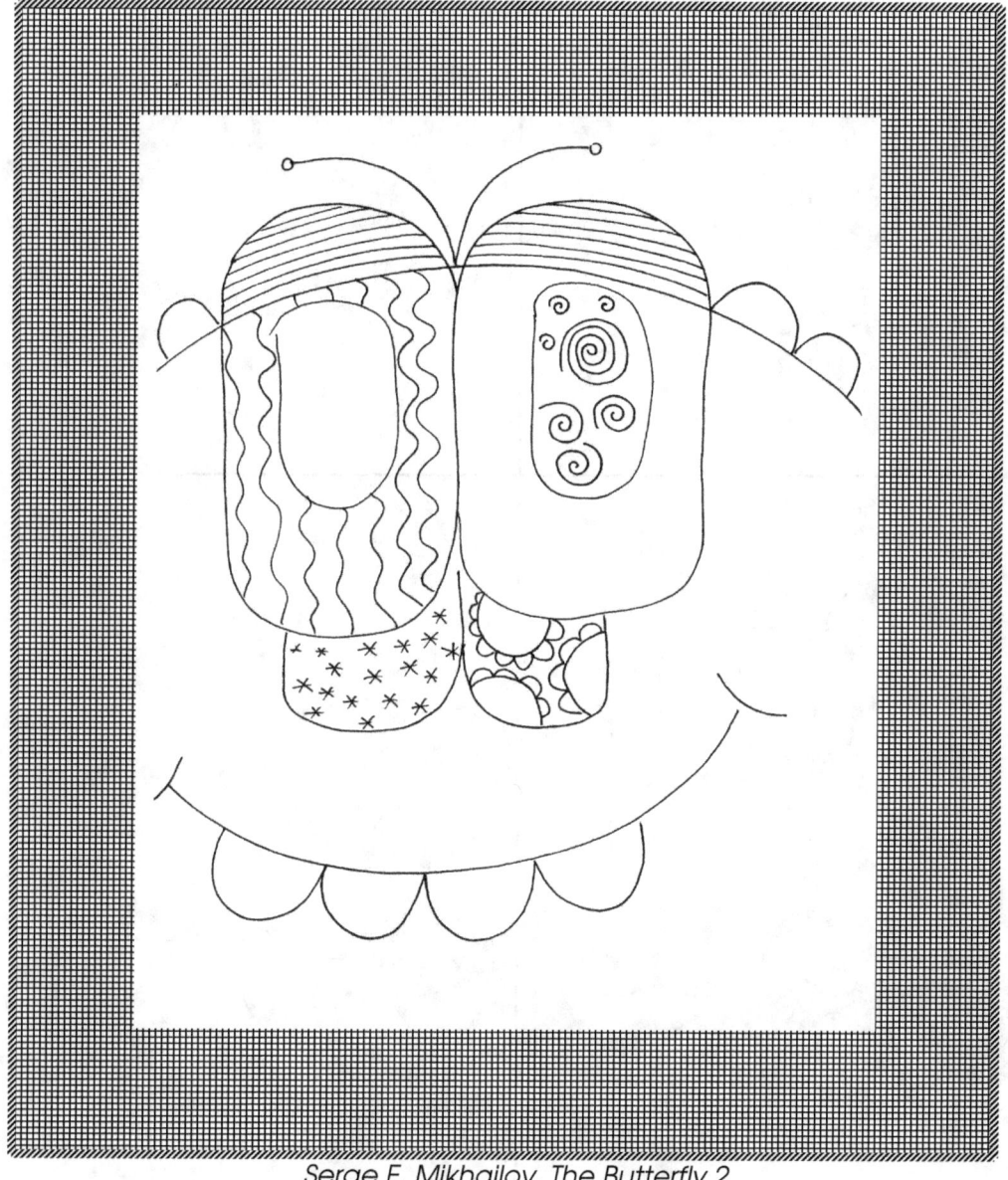

Serge E. Mikhailov, The Butterfly 2

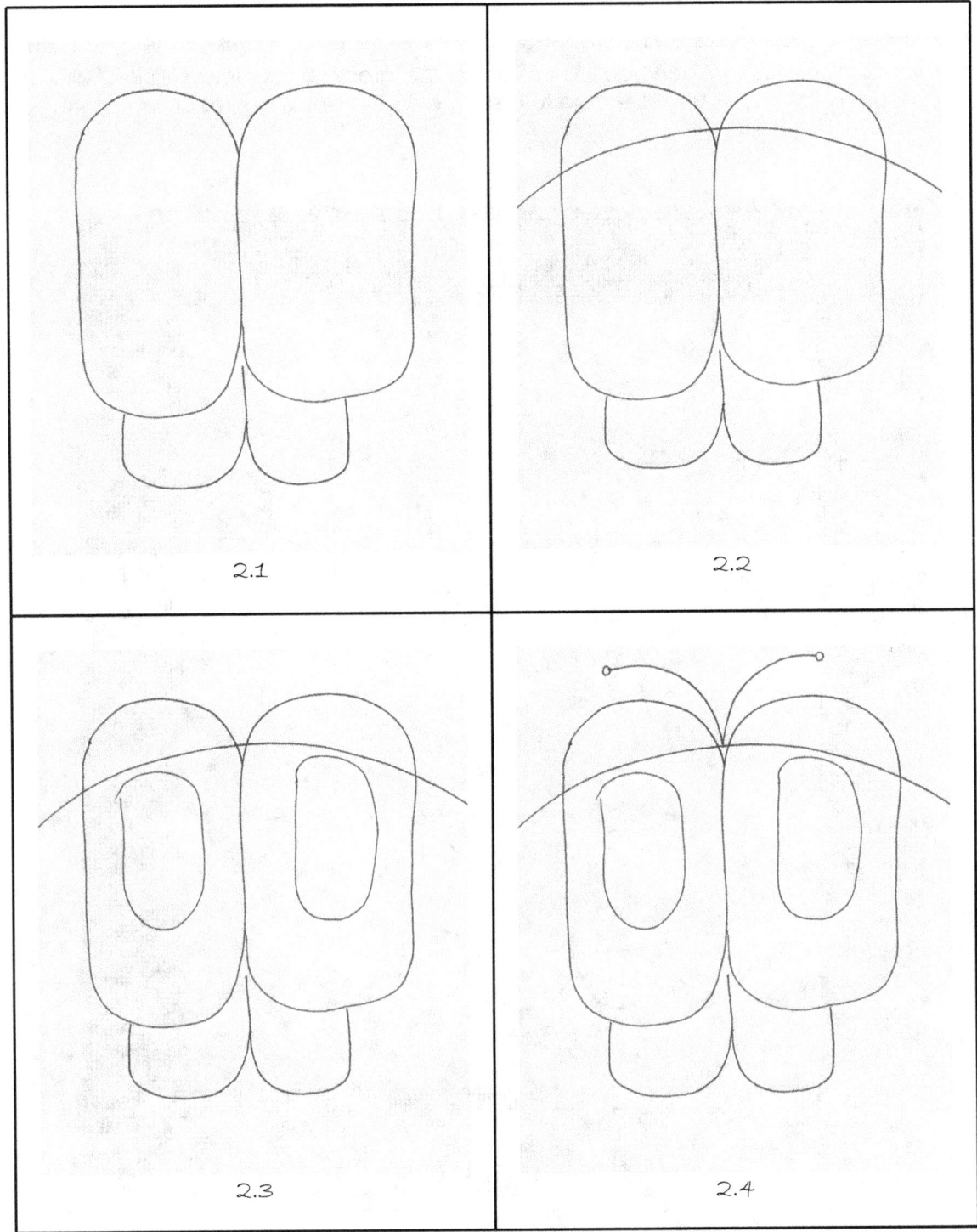

2.1

2.2

2.3

2.4

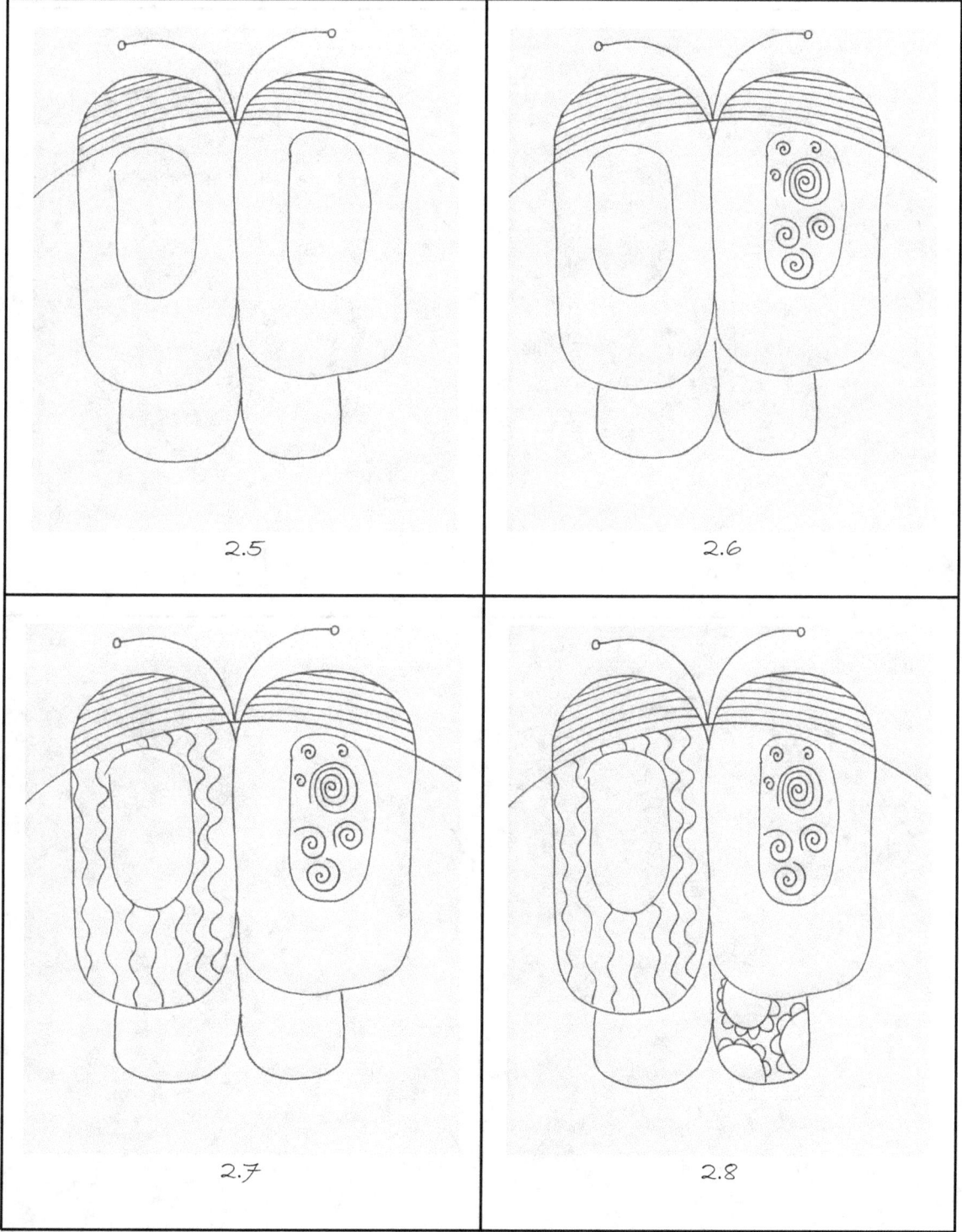

2.5

2.6

2.7

2.8

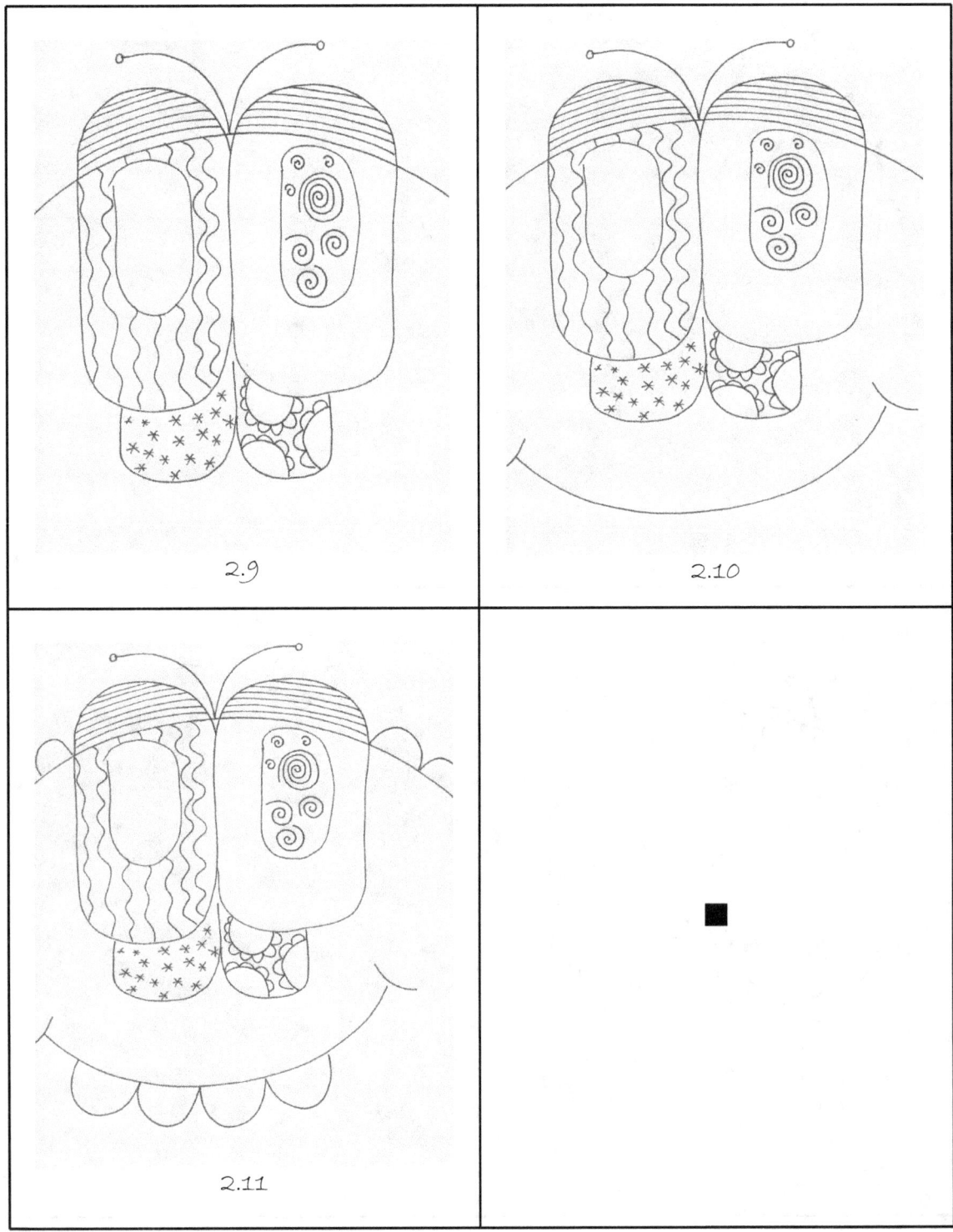

2.9

2.10

2.11

How to Draw Butterfly 3

These pages will show you how to create NeoWhimsy Butterfly 3. The butterflies' drawings, which you see in this book, show the power of imagination. They are all different and unique. Imagination is a world where images are nested in the mind to form a concept of what is not actually present to the senses. Follow the visual instructions; learn how the flowing line creates sections, and how an artist fills these sections with different repetitive patterns. You already understand the process and soon you will be able to create NeoWhimsies independently, using your imagination and artistic skills.

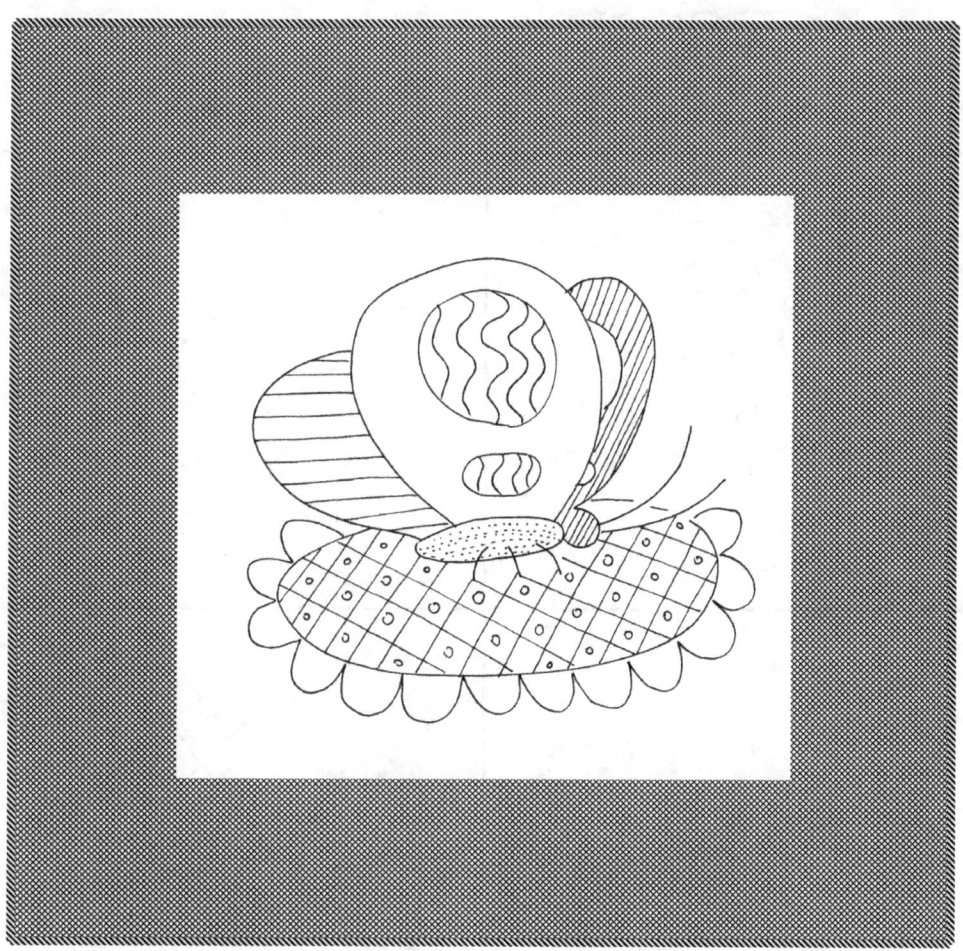

Serge E. Mikhailov, *The Butterfly 3*

This page includes the repetitive patterns, which Serge E. Mikhailov uses in his NeoWhimsy Butterfly 3.

Butterfly's contour	Flower
Waves	Strips
Dots	Squares with circles

Next visual instruction will show you how to draw NeoWhimsy Butterfly 3. Art is a marriage between craft and imagination, skills, and inventiveness coming together. When you draw often, you develop your skills, imagination and the eye, brain, hand, connection.

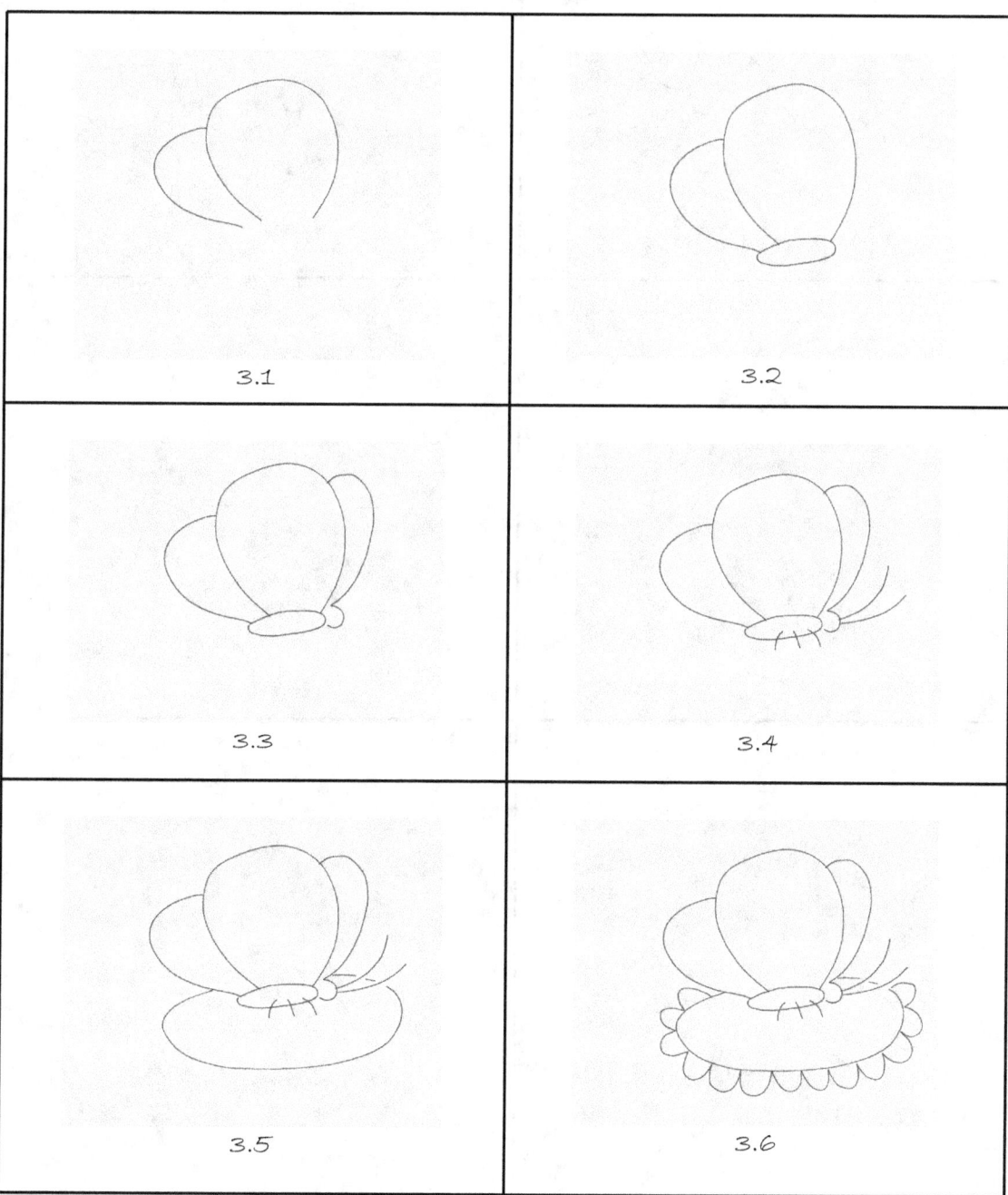

3.1

3.2

3.3

3.4

3.5

3.6

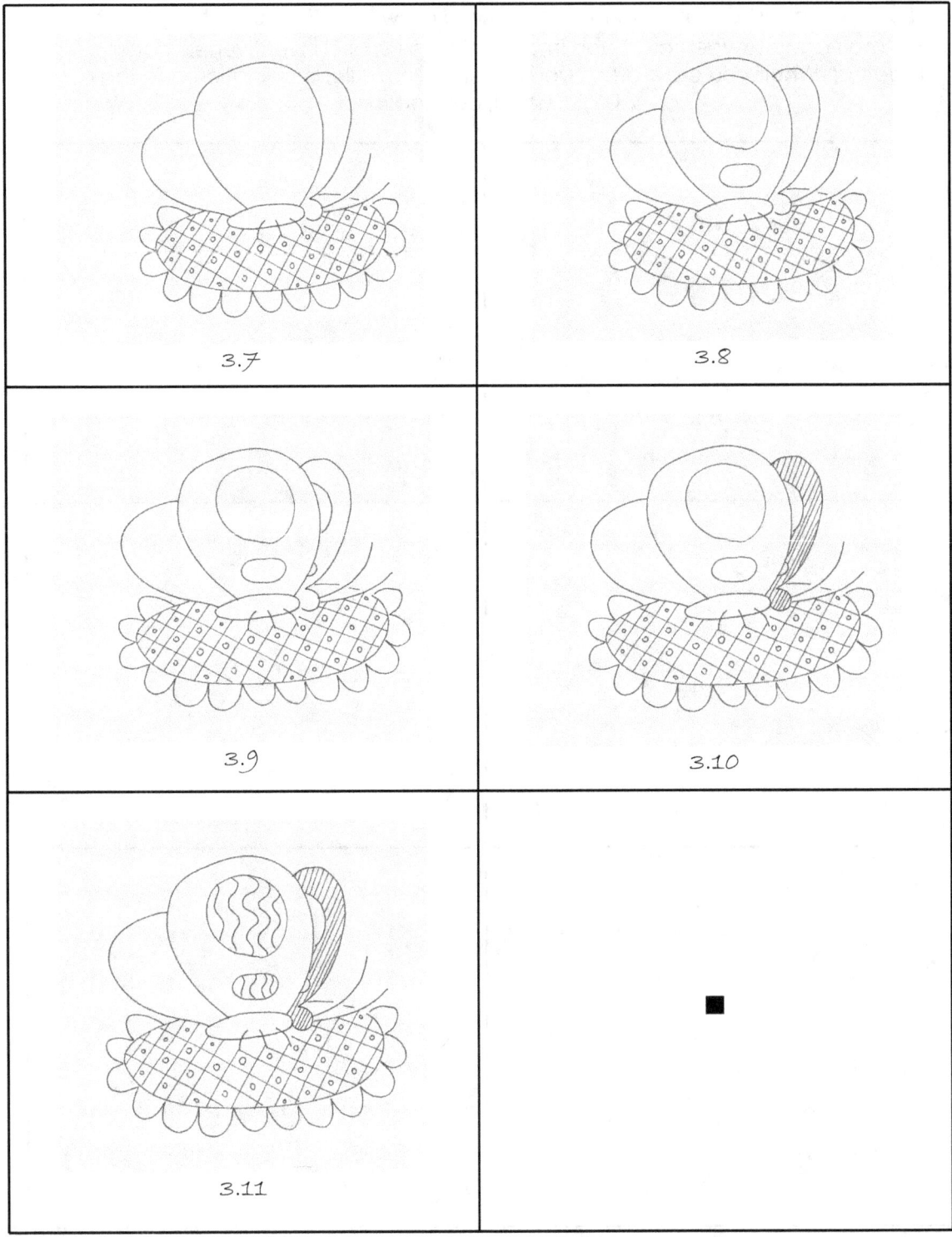

3.7

3.8

3.9

3.10

3.11

Draw the Butterflies with Serge
Here and Now

*T*he next pages your will use for your training. Get your ink pen ready and fill the sections of images of butterflies with different repetitive patterns. Use your imagination to create the new repetitive patterns; also you can use those, which you already know. Follow your creative instinct. Some section(s) you can leave blank - it is the 'air'. Every image needs the 'air' too, as us, people. Then, they are breathing. Nothing is impossible. When you draw the repetitive patterns you enter the meditative state of mind, you brain is relaxing. This drawing helps you to achieve both the interesting artistic results and purity of your mind. More you practice, better your NeoWhimsies are.

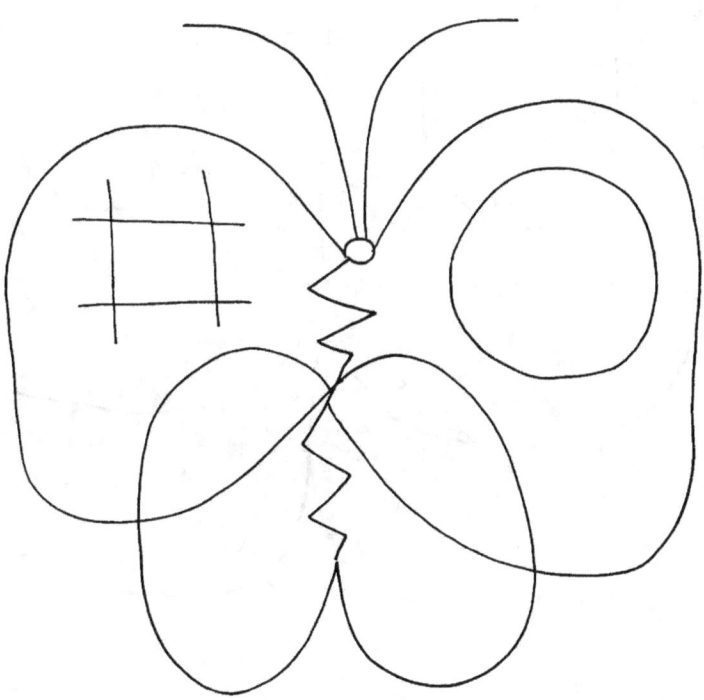

The Butterfly 1

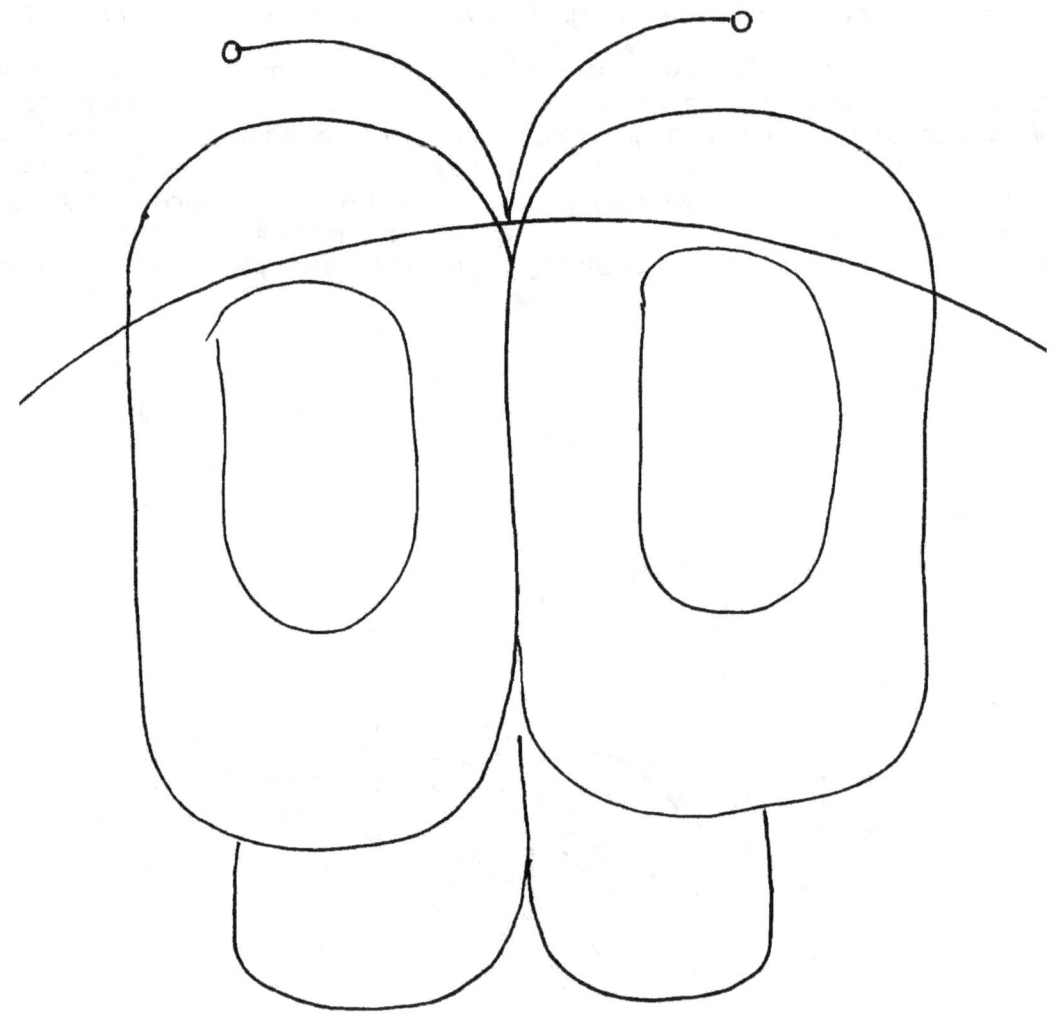

The Butterfly 2

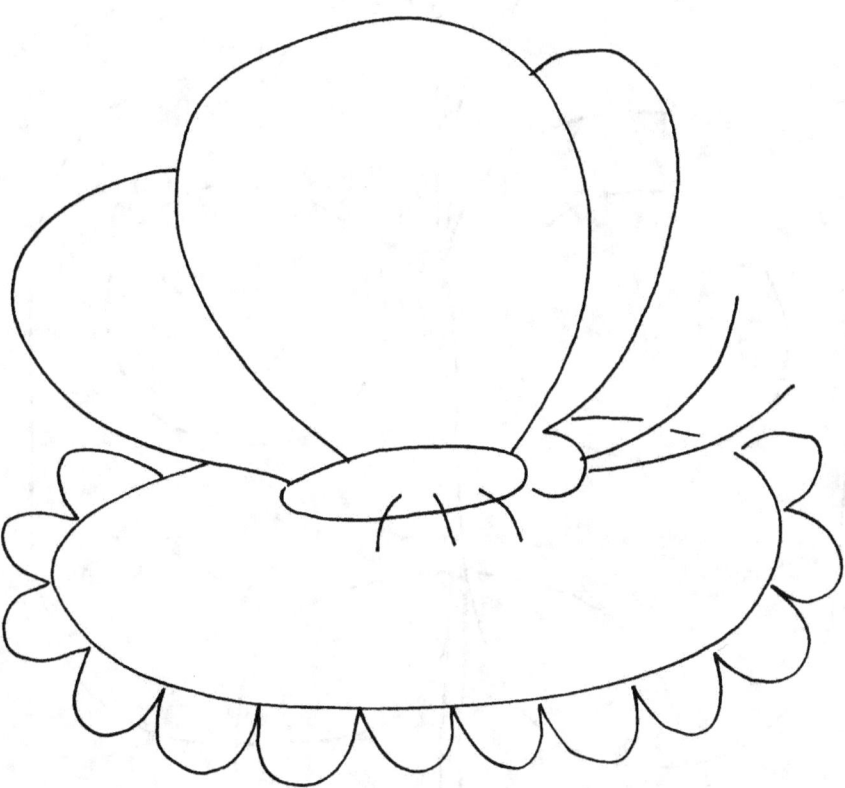

The Butterfly 3

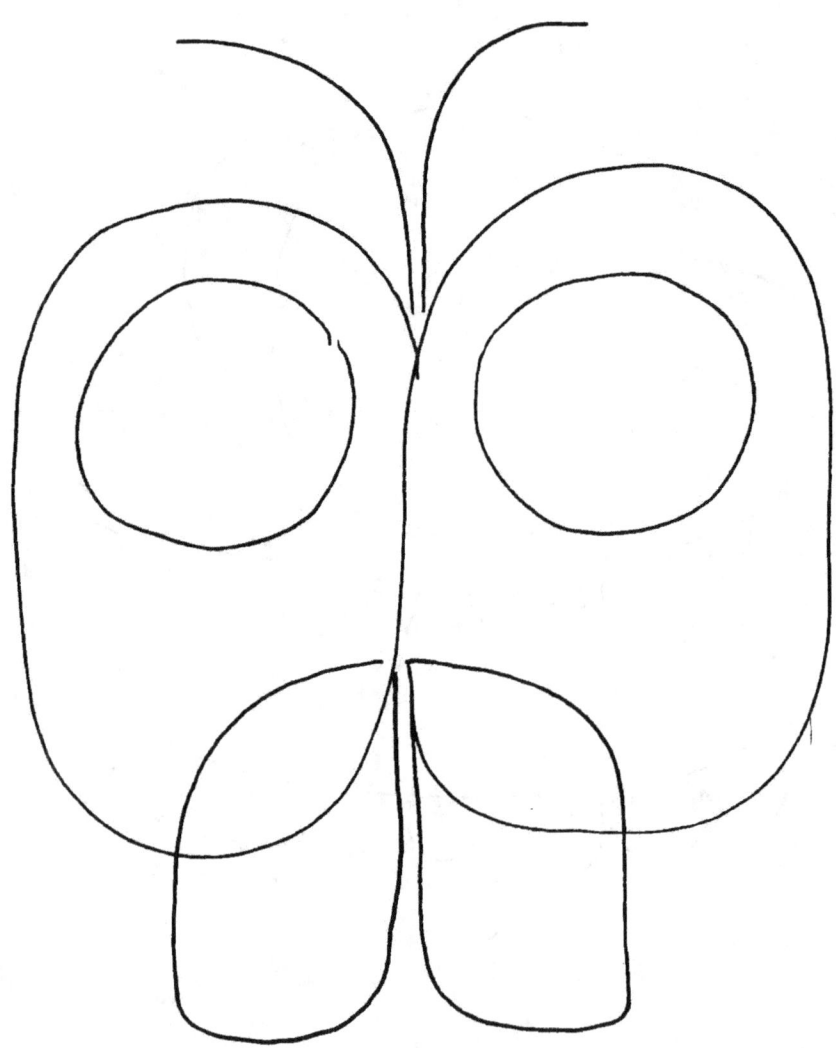

The Butterfly 4

First Steps: NeoWhimsies: NeoPopRealism Ink Drawing for Beginners

Draw the Flowers

The following pages will show you how to create the NeoWhimsies flowers. Your drawing is a reflection of your ideas. Through the line and repetitive patterns - ornaments - you are sharing your innermost thoughts, you imagination. The practicing helps you to overcome any limitations that stand in the way of achieving the result you want. Success is not about focusing just on your strengths. It is more about stretching yourself beyond your limits. Have passion and confidence. The drawing will help you learn more about yourself. If you truly want to succeed in your drawing be the best you can be. Focus on your strengths, skills, and self-improvement, be open for training, and turn your new skills into the new strengths. Think of limitation you have as the challenges, not weaknesses. Your attitude can change everything. When you draw NeoWhimsies, you use the line and different repetitive patterns. Each flower has different character and created using different shapes and patterns. The visual instructions will lead you from the beginning to end of the drawing process. Every following image includes new detail(s). The final images look like this:

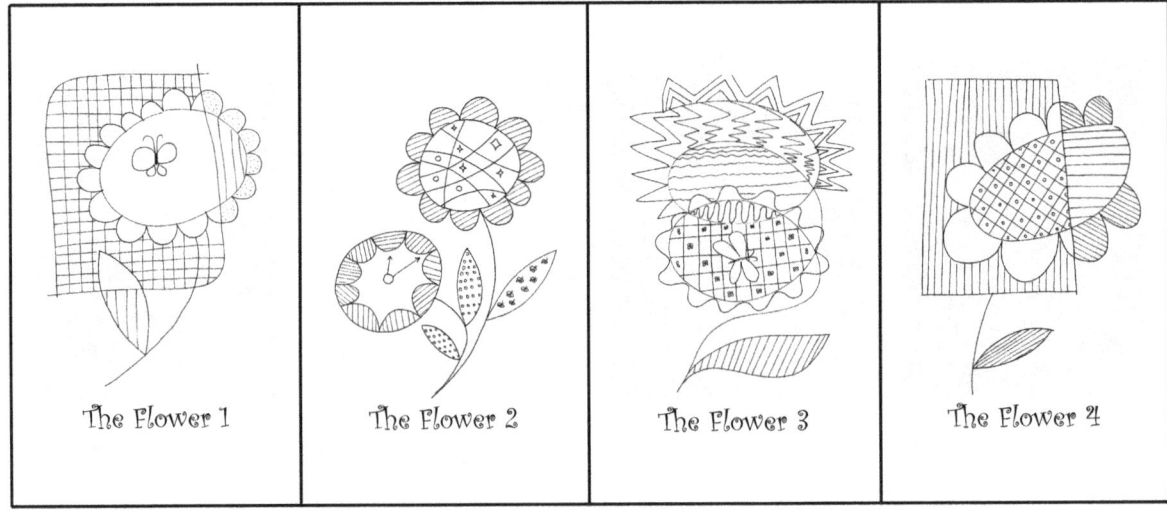

The Flower 1   The Flower 2   The Flower 3   The Flower 4

How to Draw Flower 1

This page includes the patterns used in NeoWhimsy Flower 1.

Strips	Dots
Squares	Flower
The fly	

Next visual instructions will show you step-by-step how to draw NeoWhimsy Flower 1. The drawings are like music - happy or sad, mysterious or straight forward, simple or complicated. . . They reflect vision and feelings of the artists who create them.

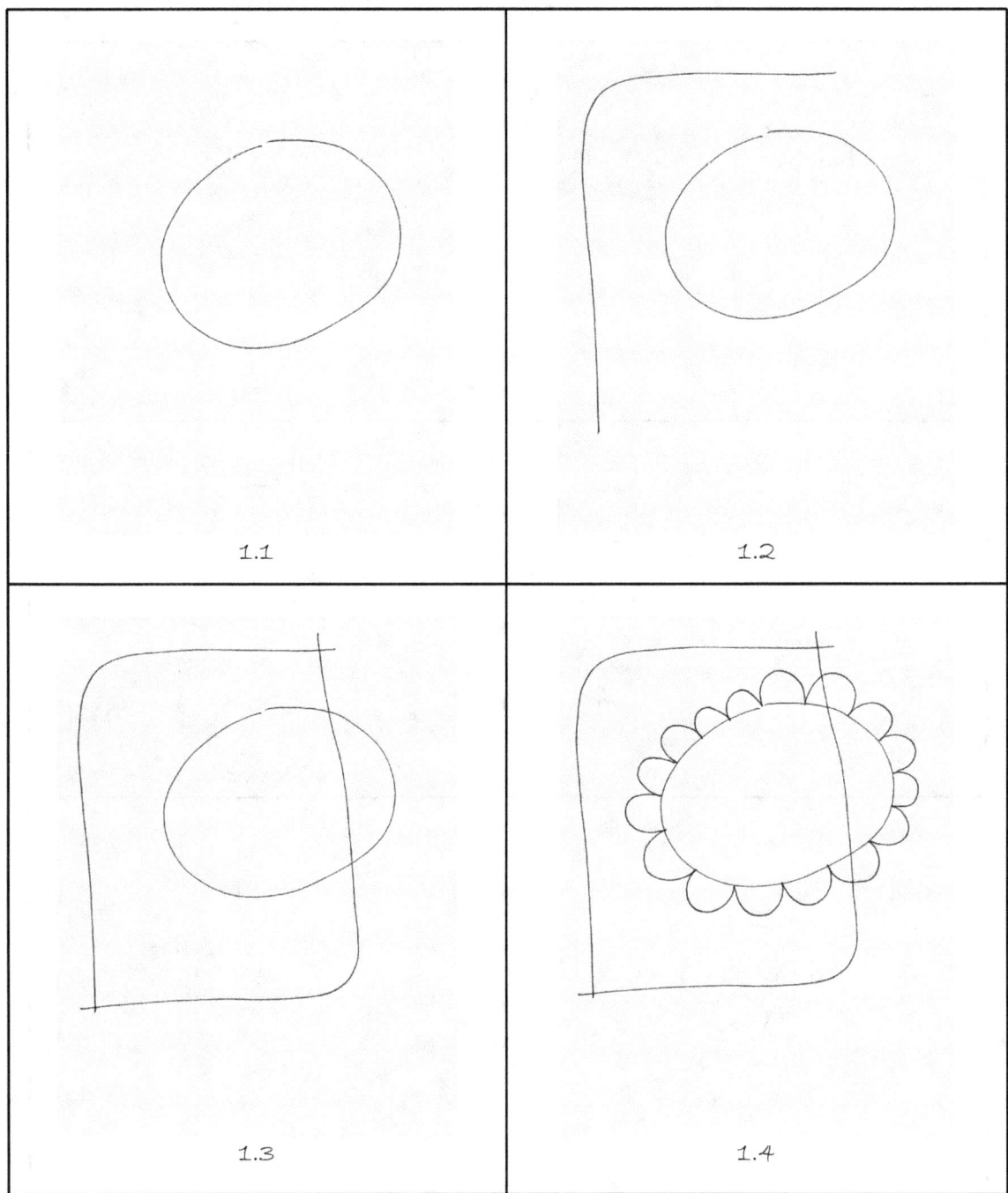

1.1

1.2

1.3

1.4

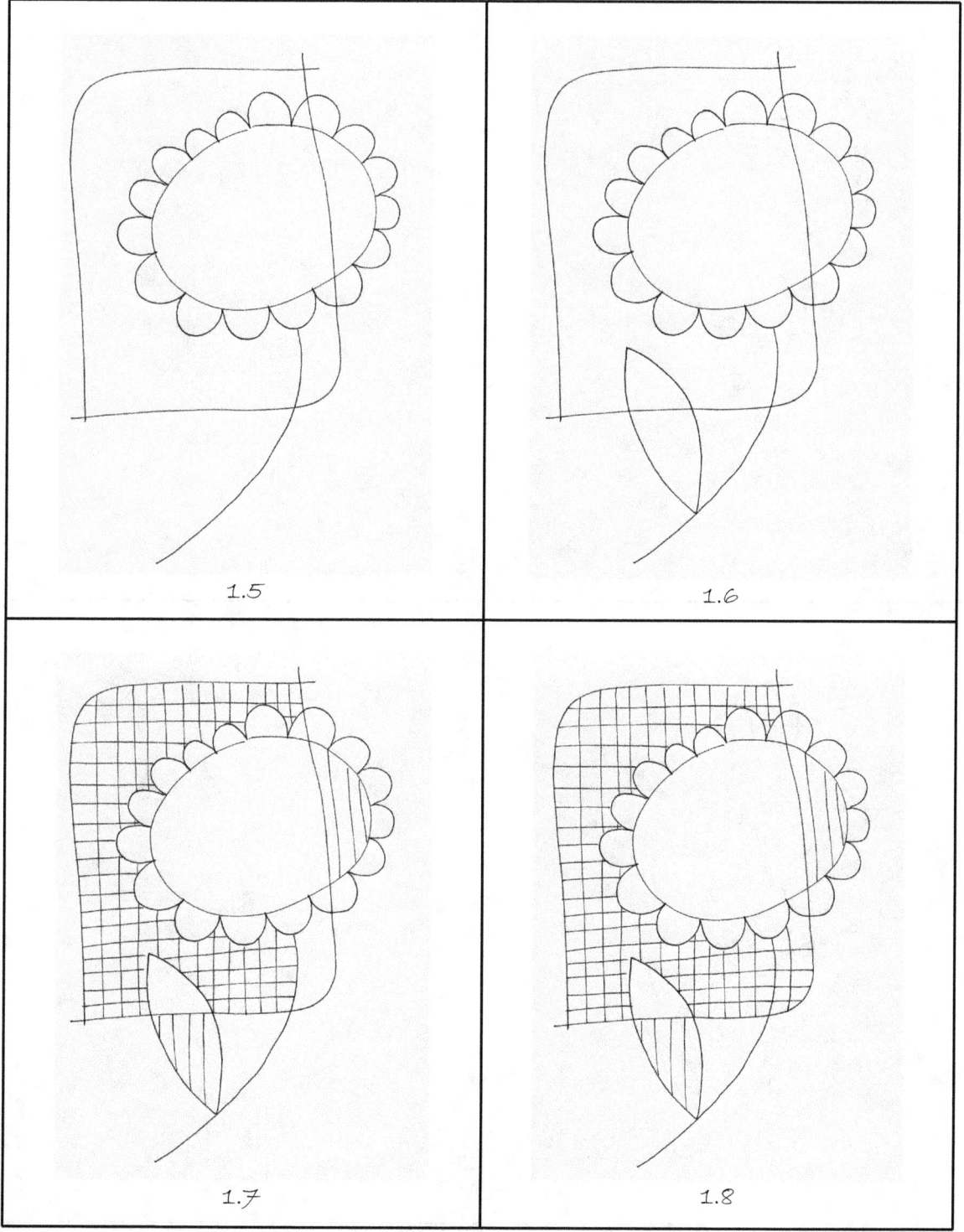

1.5

1.6

1.7

1.8

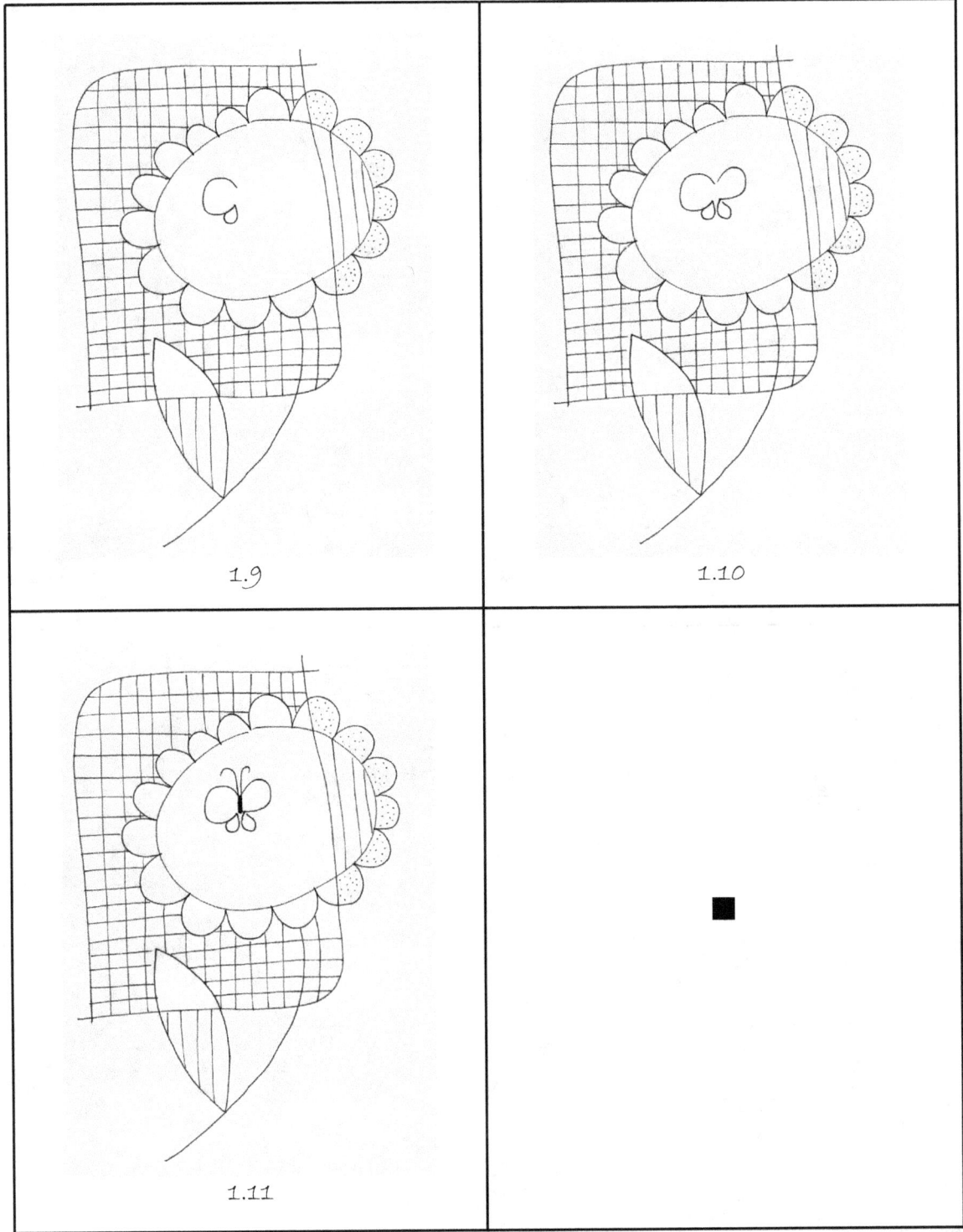

1.9

1.10

1.11

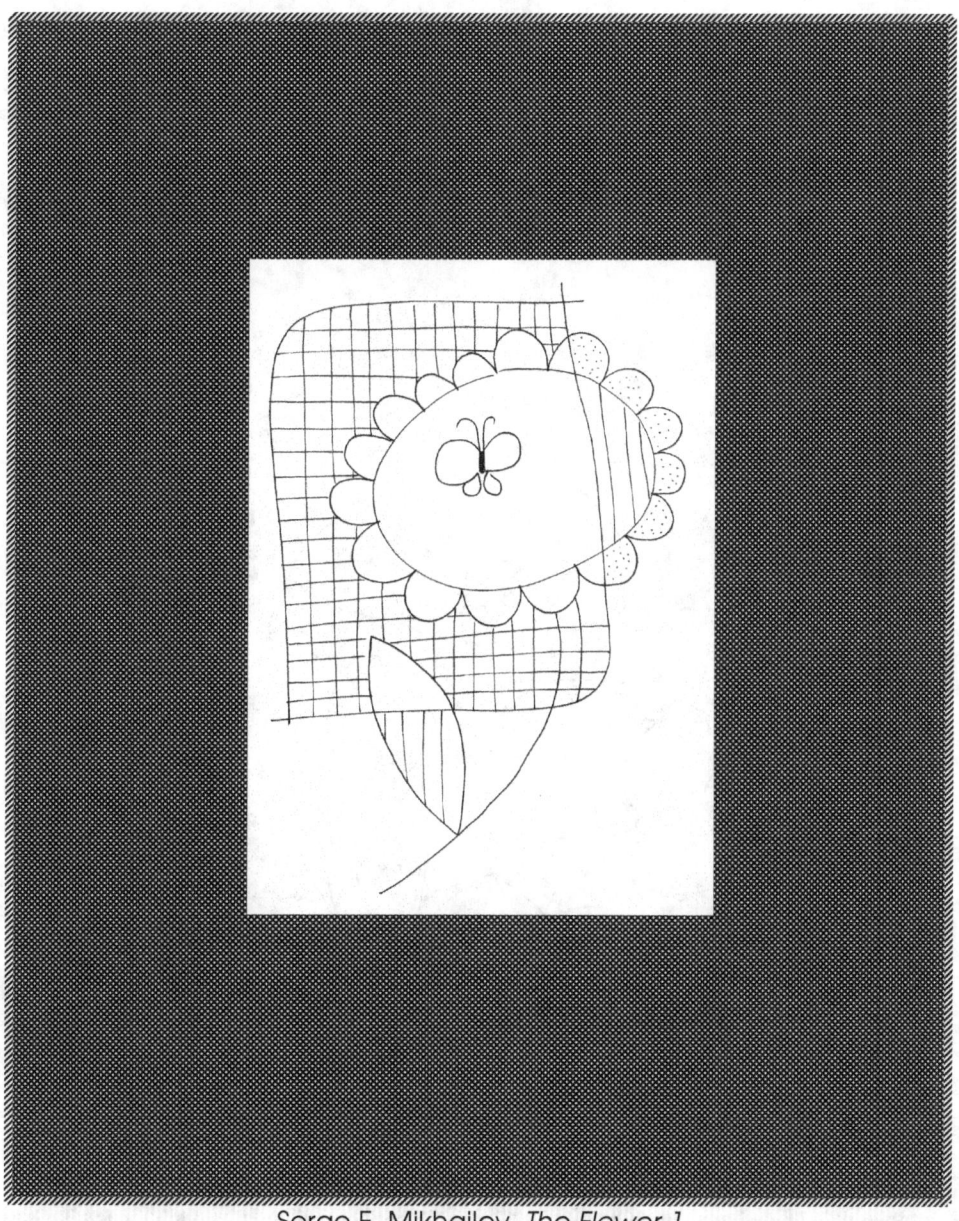

Serge E. Mikhailov, *The Flower 1*

How to Draw Flower 2

Our world is fast, challenging, demanding, exciting. It produces anxiety and stress. Everything is transforming every minute right before your eyes, it is waiting for you to get on board. Do not resist new ideas, open your mind and explore what is possible, employing your talent and skills. Learn, create, meditate!

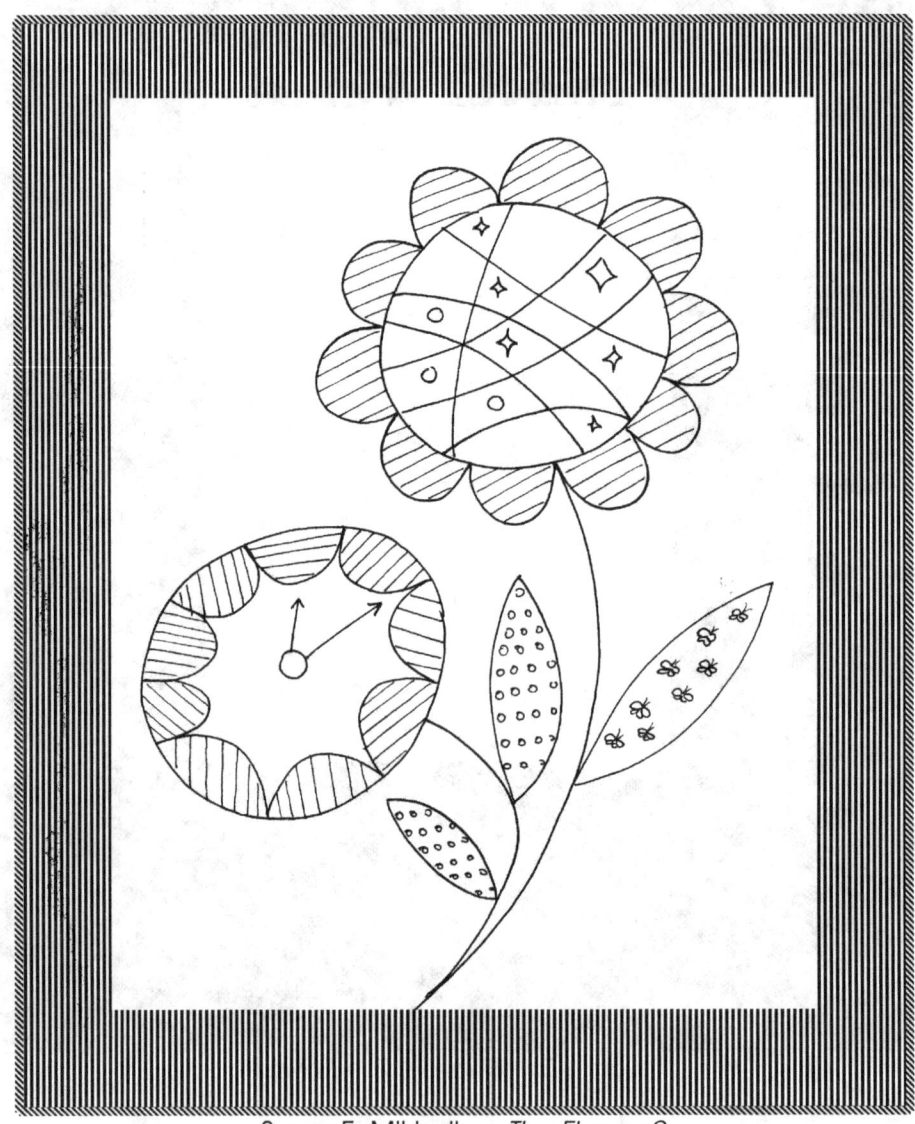

Serge E. Mikhailov, *The Flower 2*

Learn about the patterns, which Serge E. Mikhailov uses in the Flower 2.

Strips	Circles
Flower	Clock
Diamonds	The Flies

Next pages contain the visual instructions, which will show you how to create NeoWhimsy Flower 2 from the beginning to end. You will learn step-by-step the developing process of the drawing. Practice and you will draw your NeoWhimsies with ease, your line will flow smooth and the compositions of your artworks will be more and more interesting and imaginative.

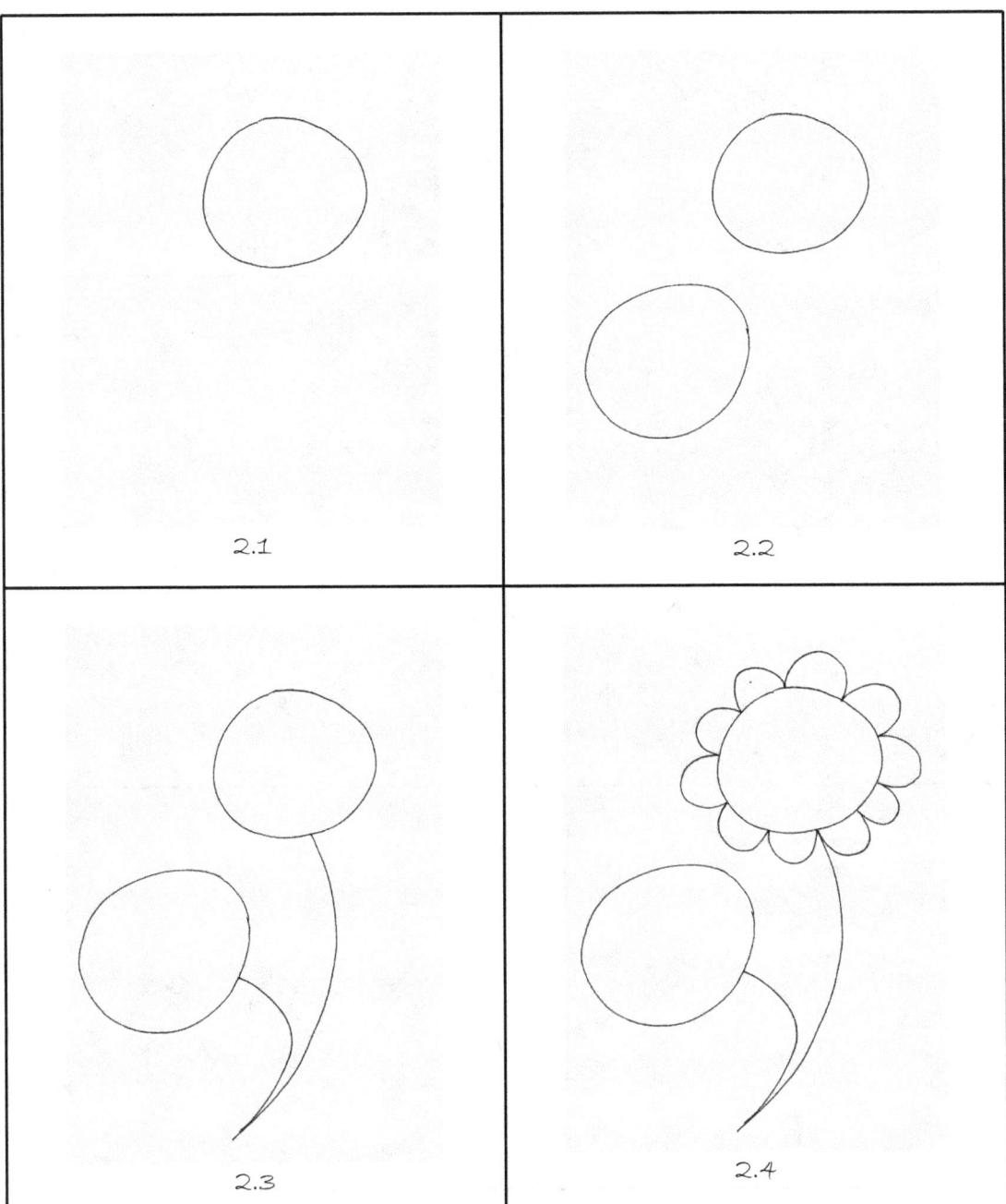

2.1

2.2

2.3

2.4

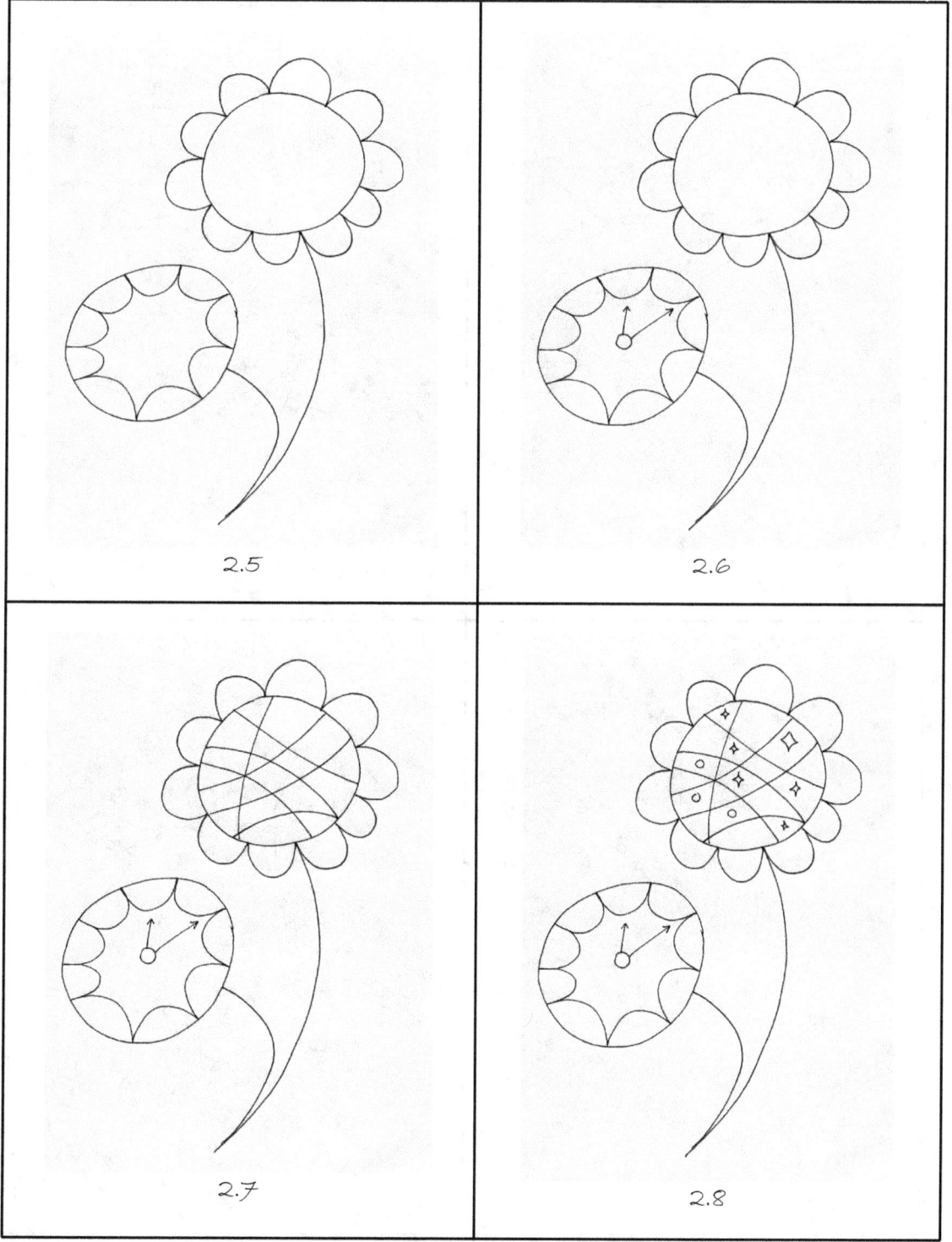

2.5

2.6

2.7

2.8

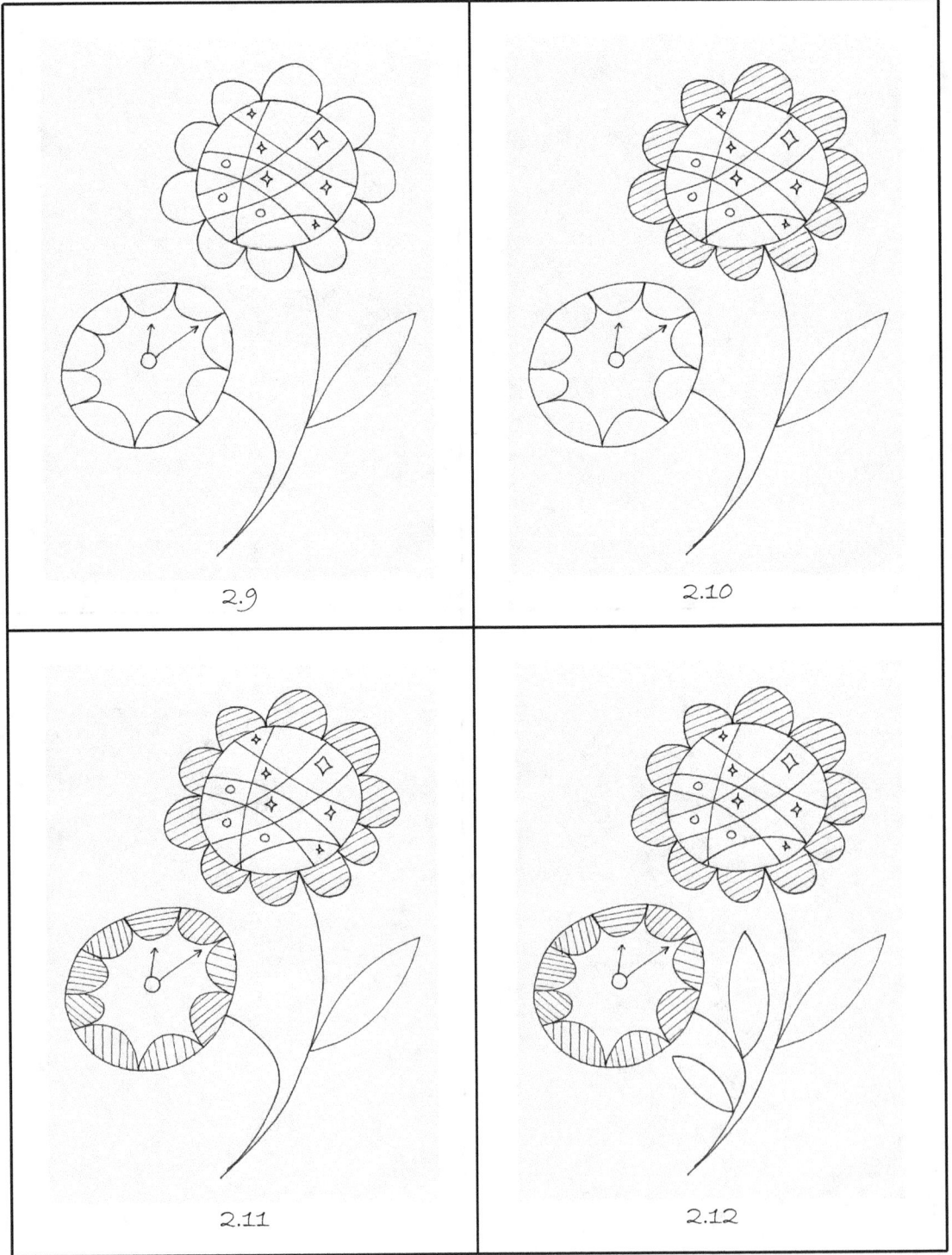

2.9

2.10

2.11

2.12

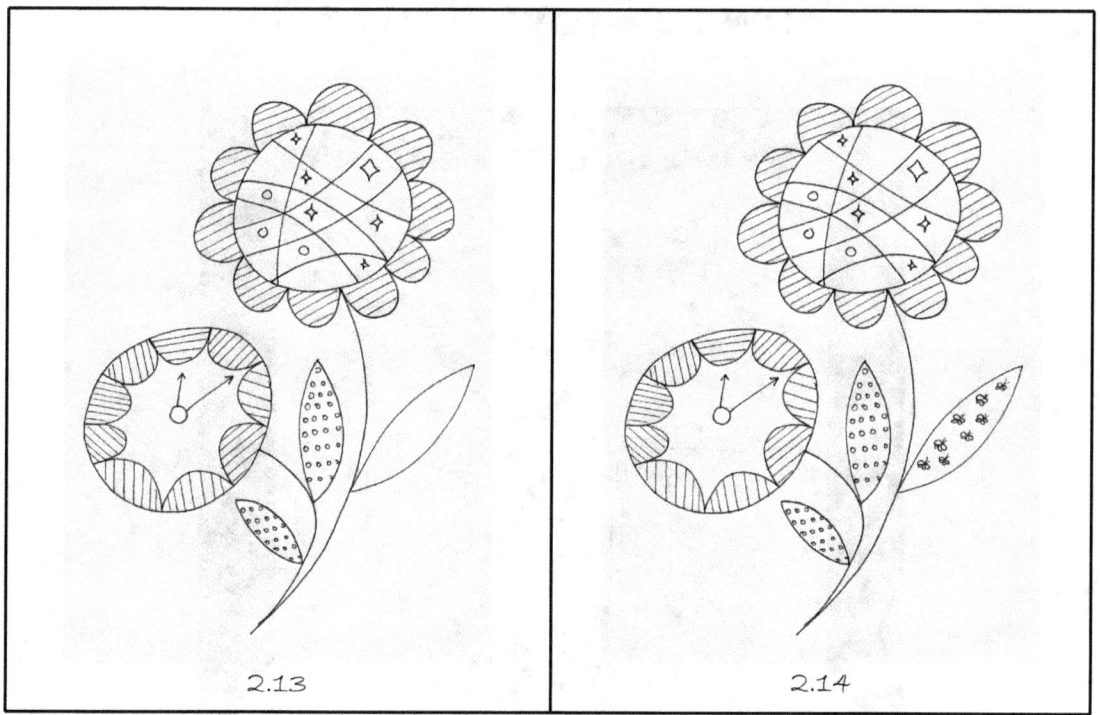

2.13   2.14

How to Draw Flower 3

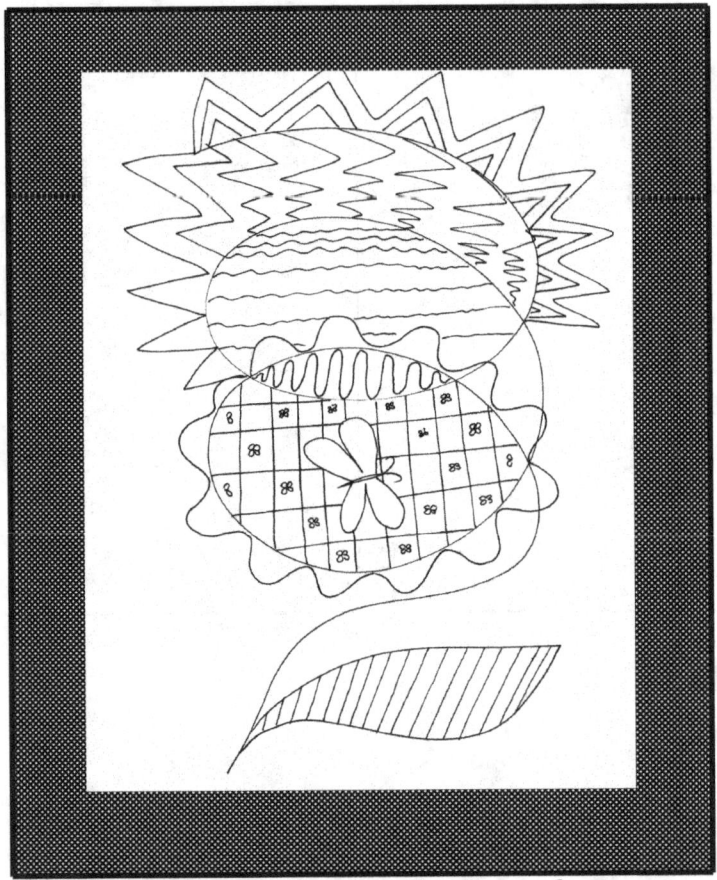

Serge E. Mikhailov, *The Flower 3*

Learn how to draw the repetitive patterns used in NeoWhimsy *Flower 3*.

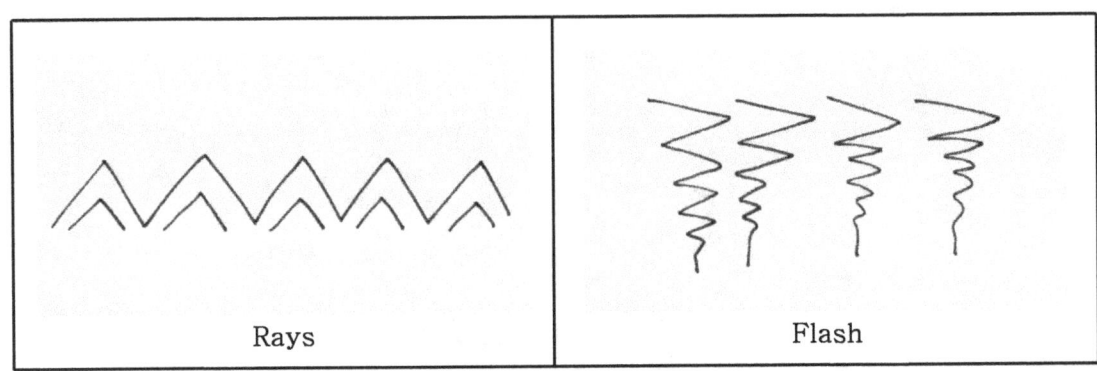

Rays   Flash

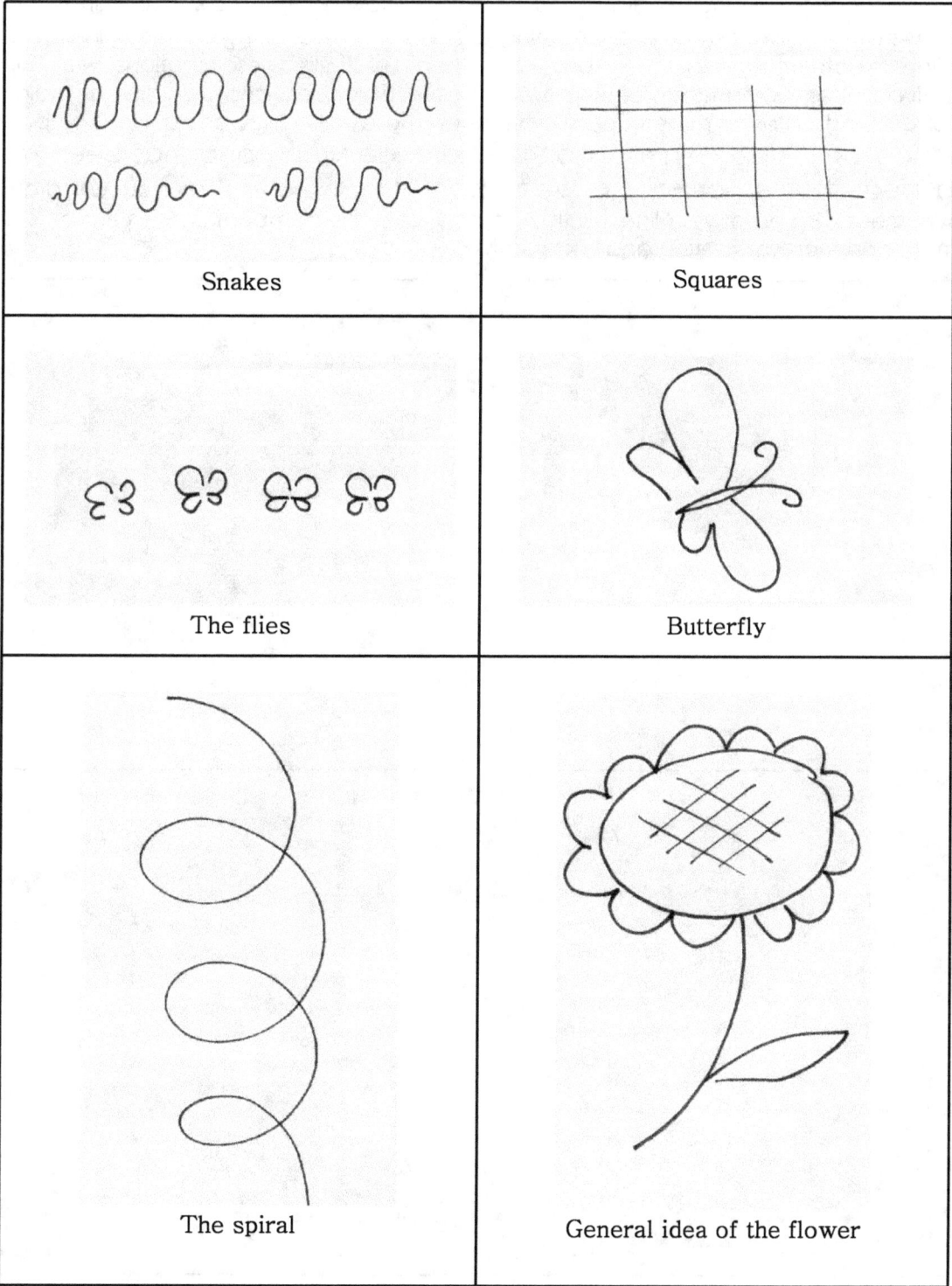

Snakes	Squares
The flies	Butterfly
The spiral	General idea of the flower

Next pages offer you the visual instructions, which show how to draw NeoWhimsy Flower 3. Step-by-step, you will learn the developing process of the drawing from beginning to end. The line creates the shapes-sections, and then artist fills these sections with different repetitive patterns-ornaments. Learn to create the balanced and beautiful combinations. These drawings are asymmetrical. Creation of these drawings could be compared to Syncopation in Jazz. Syncopation is where the strong beat has been moved to a beat that is normally a weak beat. Practice and soon you will draw your NeoWhimsies with ease, your line will flow smooth and the compositions of your artworks will be more and more interesting and imaginative.

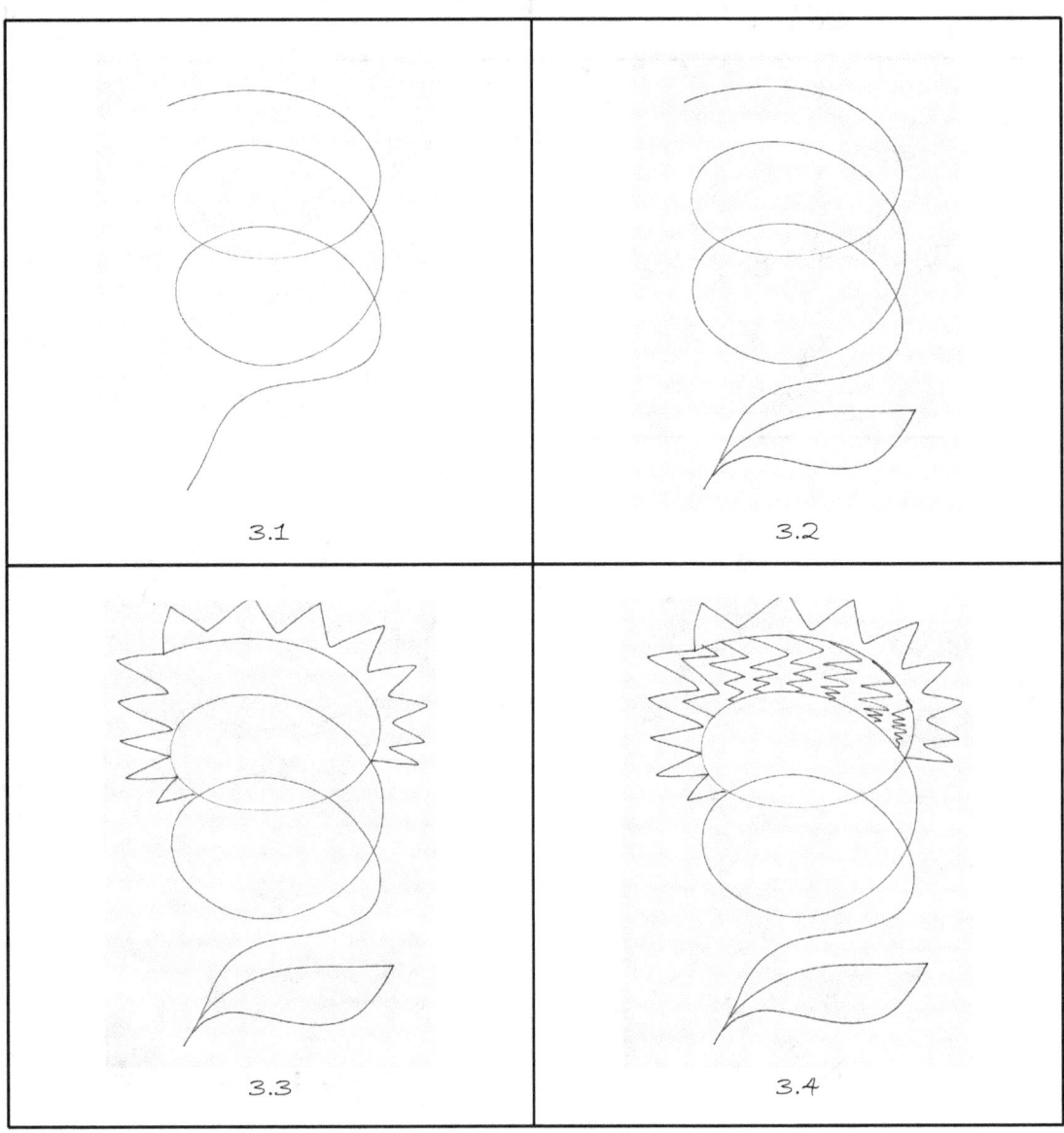

3.1

3.2

3.3

3.4

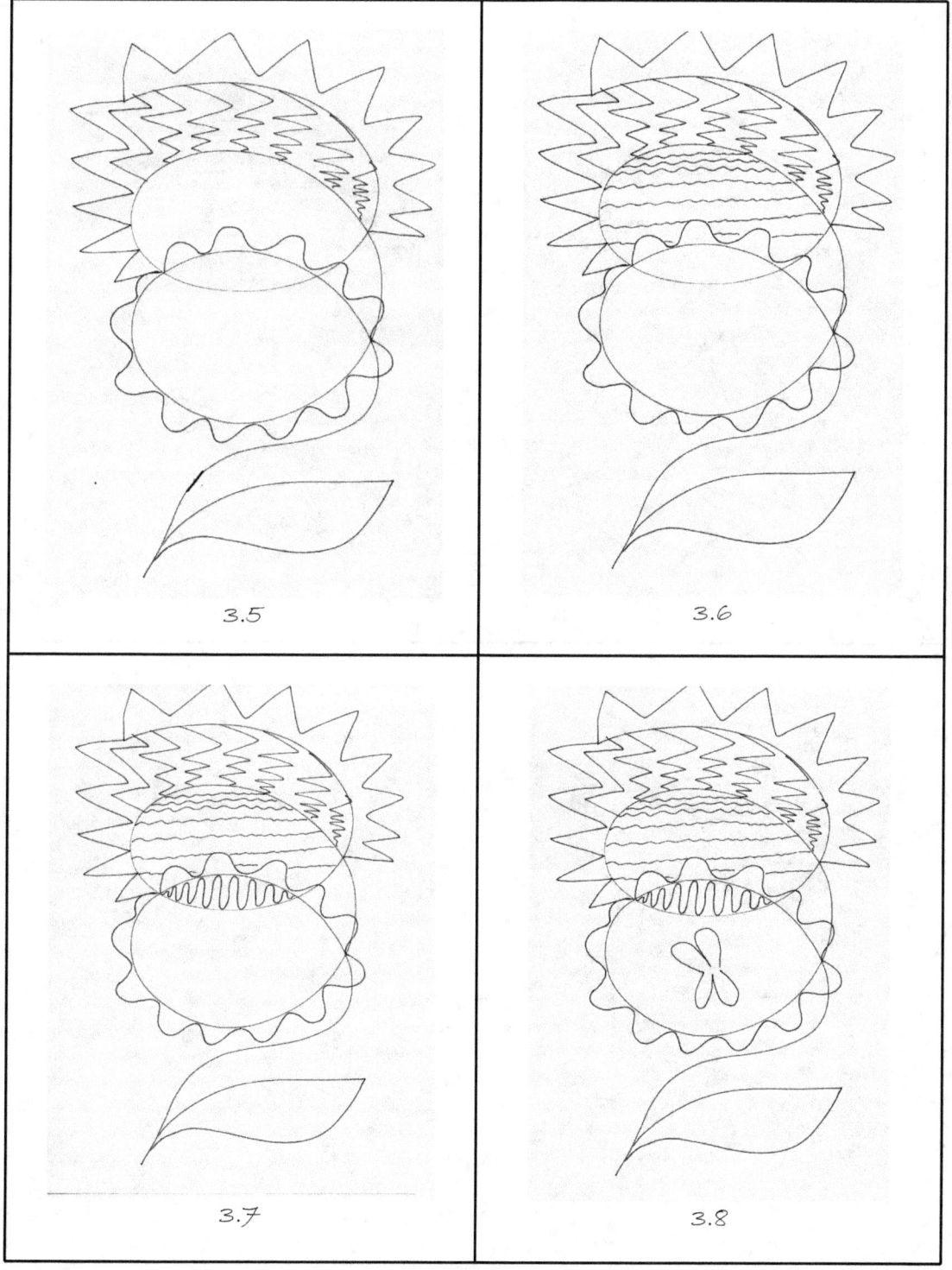

3.5

3.6

3.7

3.8

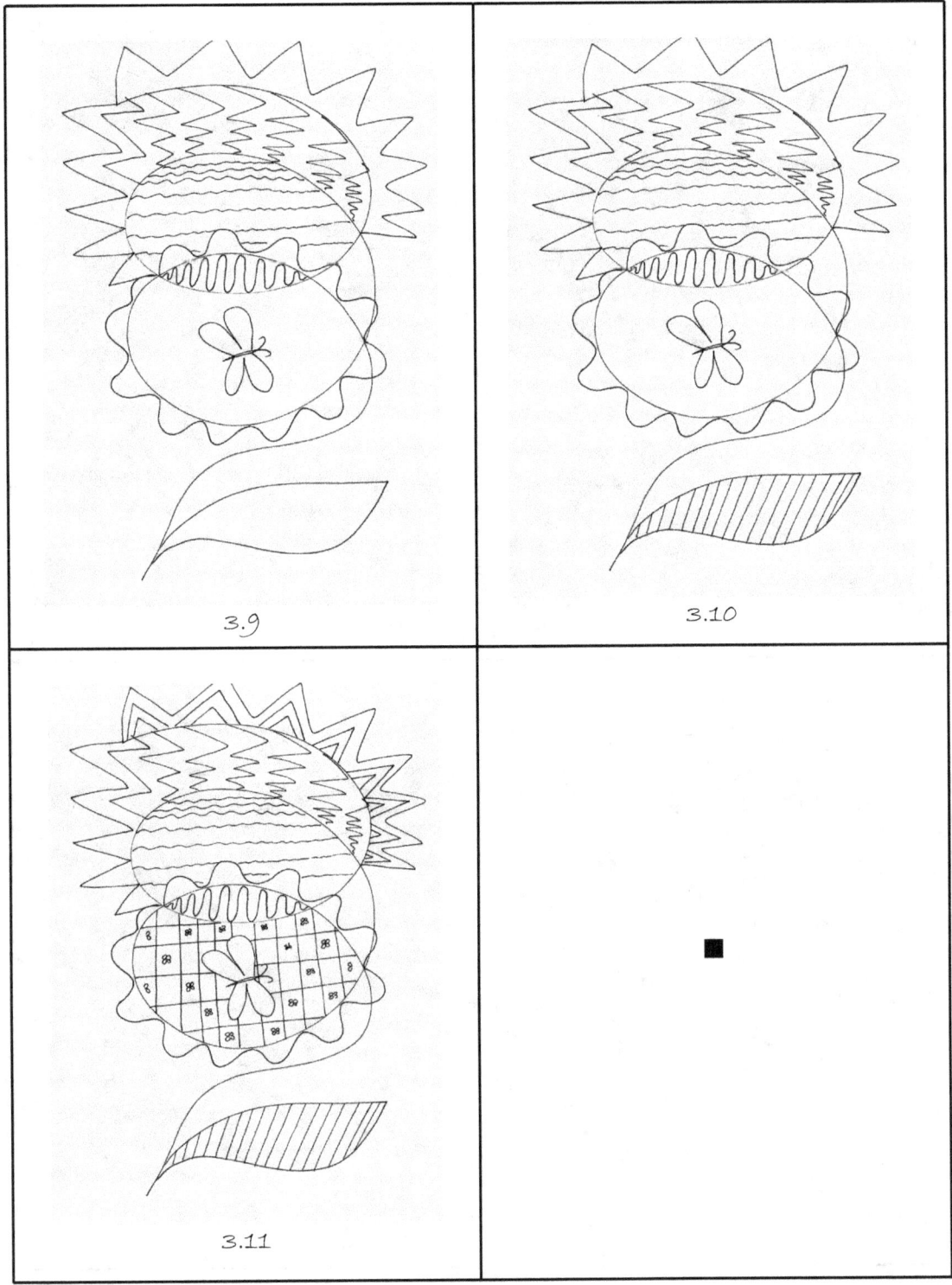

3.9

3.10

3.11

How to Draw Flower 4

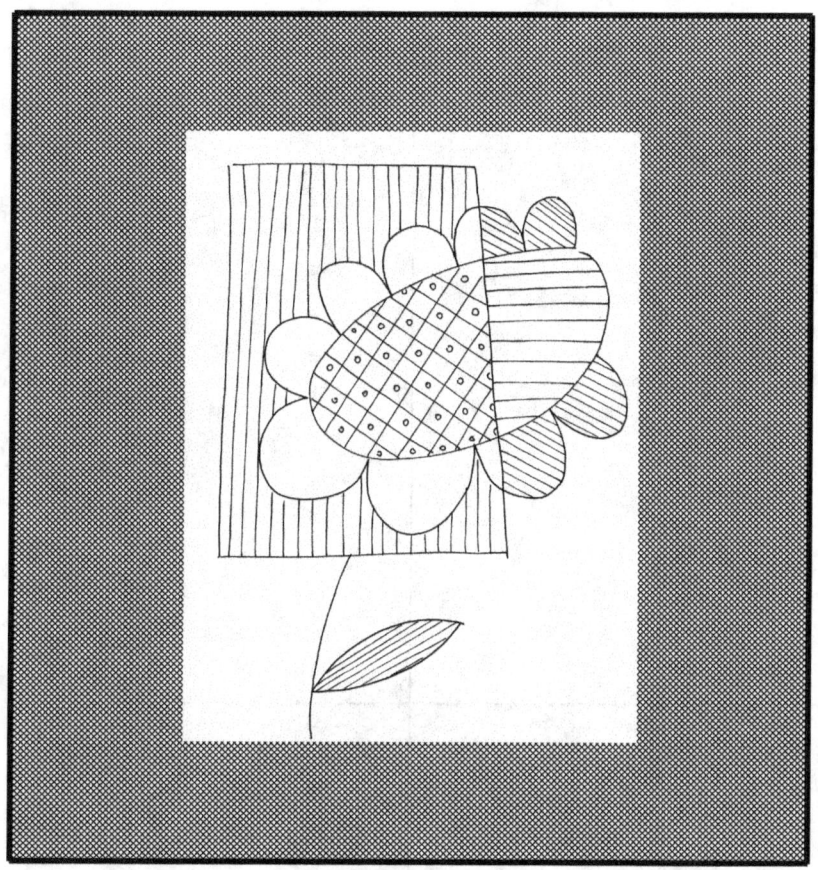

Serge E. Mikhailov, *The Flower 4*

The following patterns are used in NeoWhimsy Flower 4:

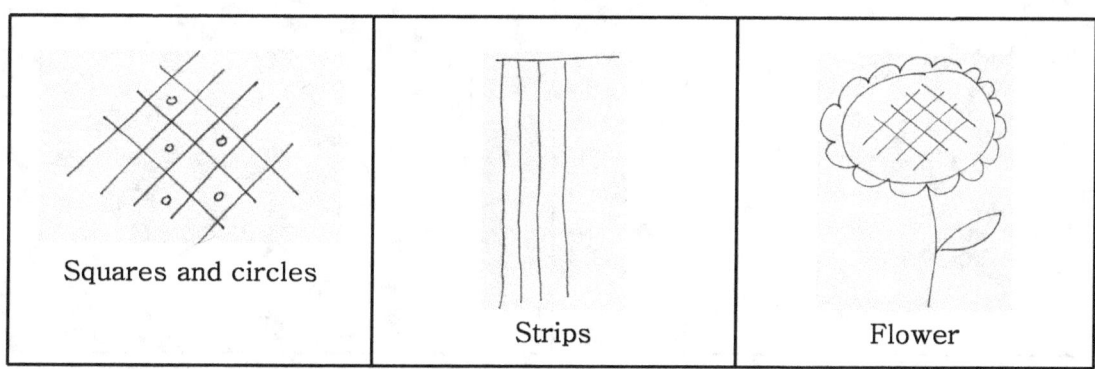

Squares and circles

Strips

Flower

The following pages include the visual instructions and show step-by-step how to draw NeoWhimsy Flower 4. The easy flowing line creates the shapes-sections, and then artist fills the sections with different repetitive patterns-ornaments.

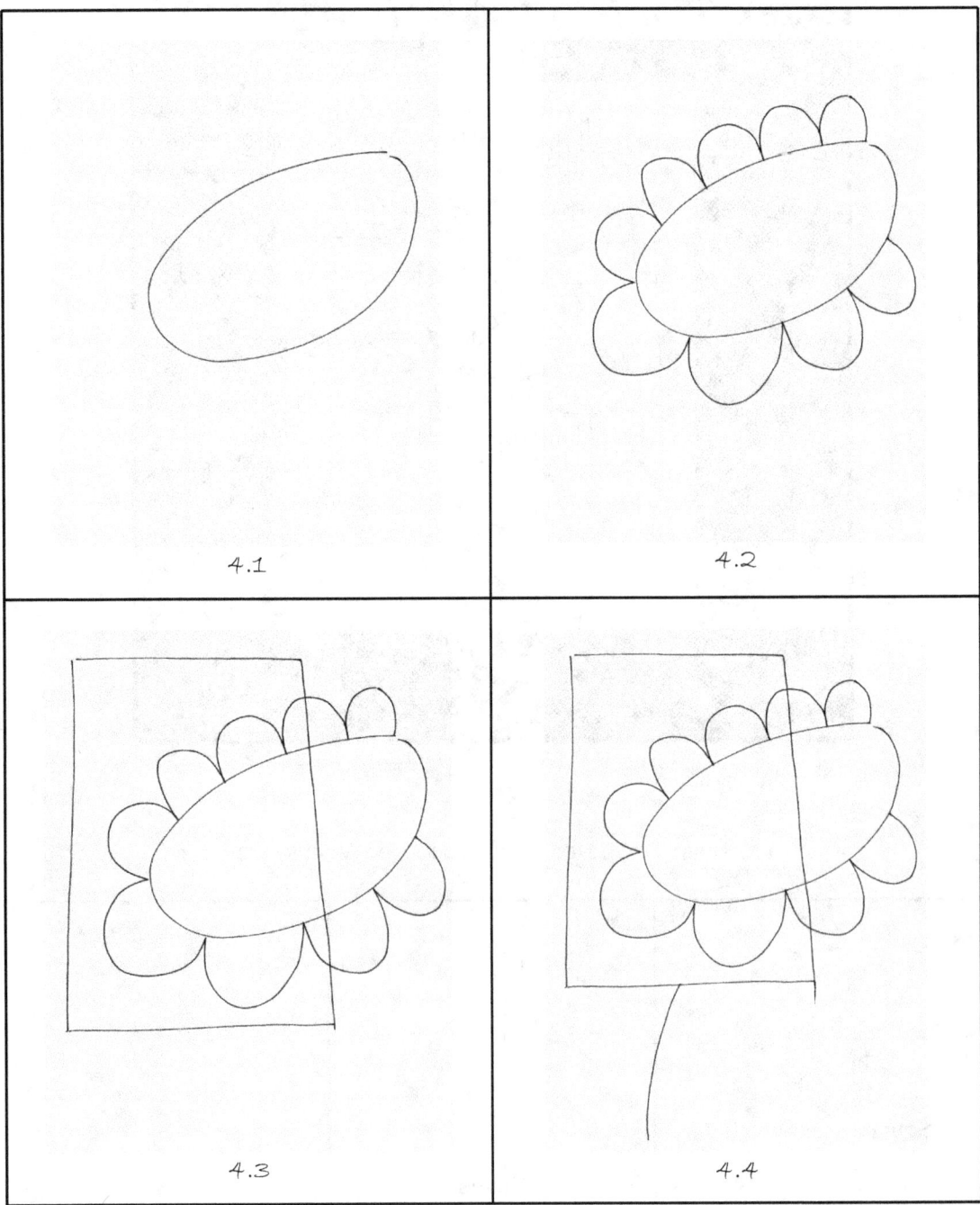

4.1

4.2

4.3

4.4

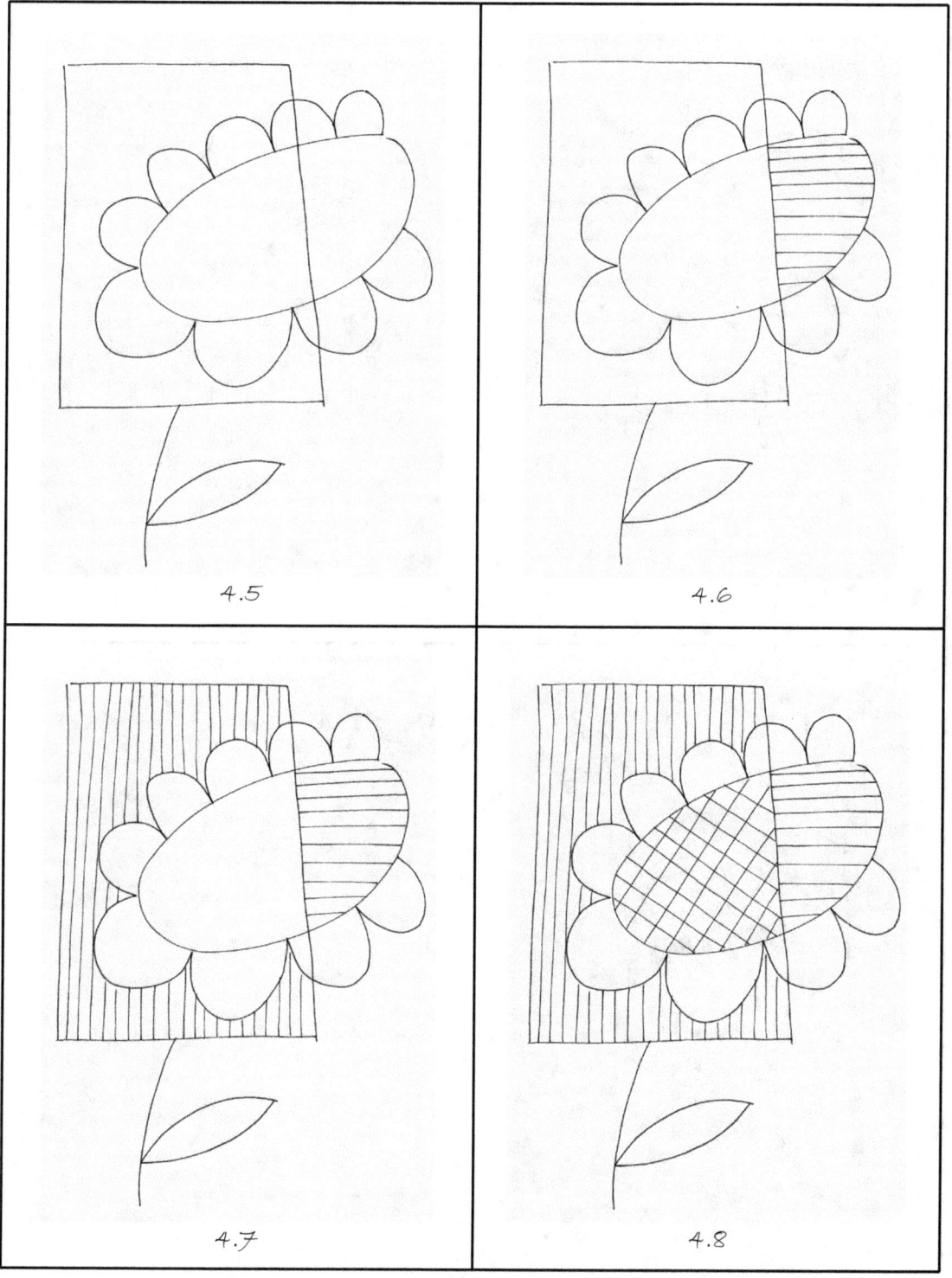

4.5

4.6

4.7

4.8

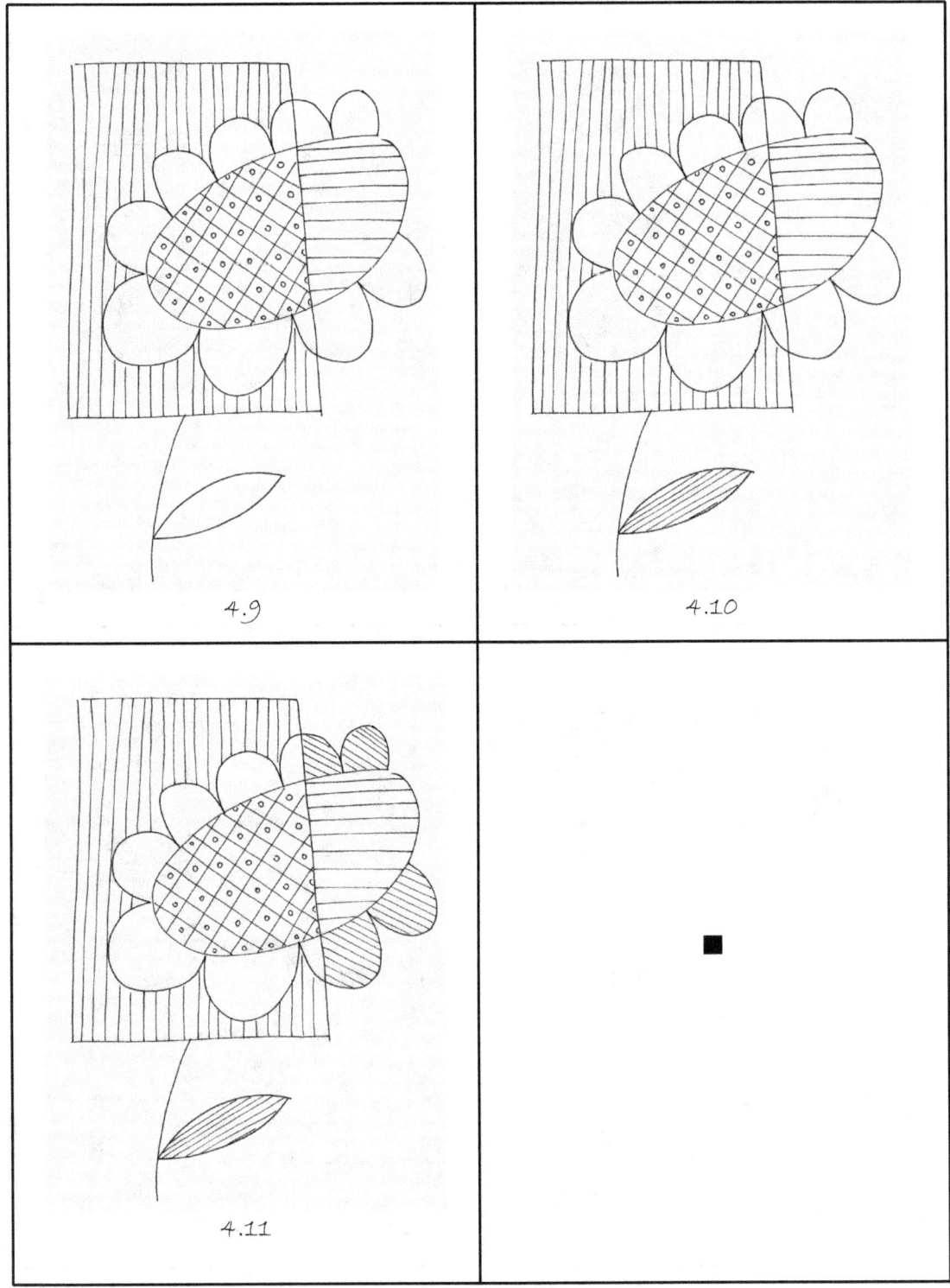

4.9

4.10

4.11

Draw the Flowers with Serge Here and Now

Draw the following NeoWhimsies with Serge. He has prepared for you the base, the "skeletons", and you should complete these artworks, putting some "meat" on the "bones". Do not copy NeoWhimsies, which you see in this book. Use your imagination, employ your skill and create absolutely new and unique drawings. Remember that imagination and inventiveness are necessary aspects of any creativity.

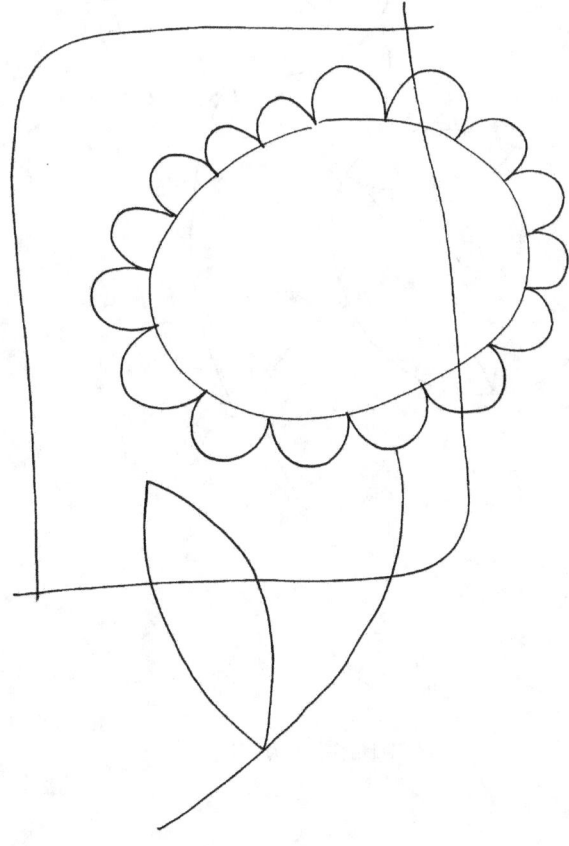

The Flower 1

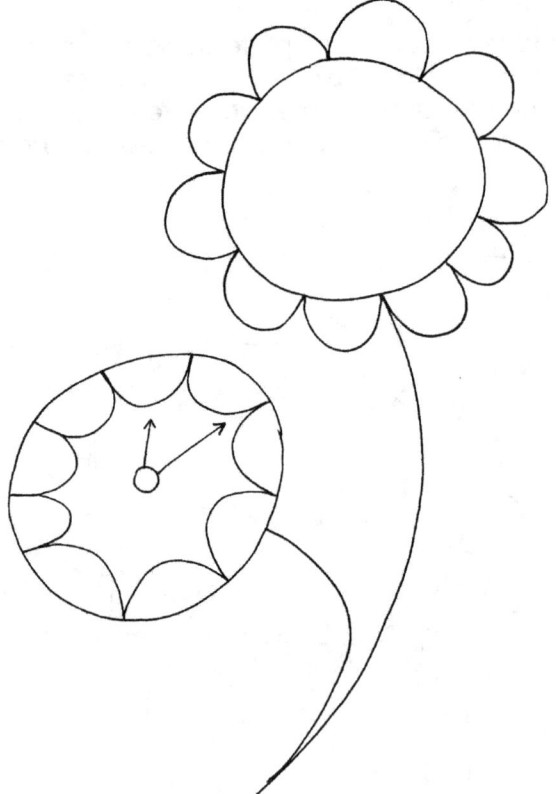

The Flower 2

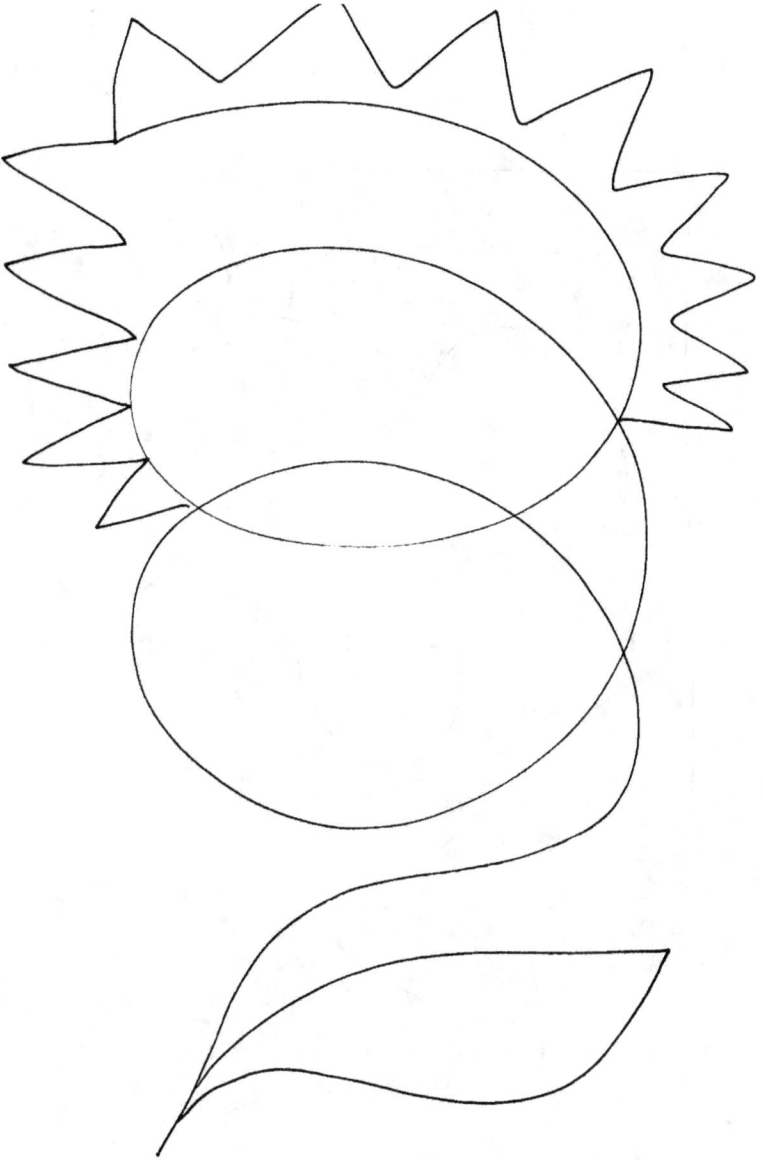

The Flower 3

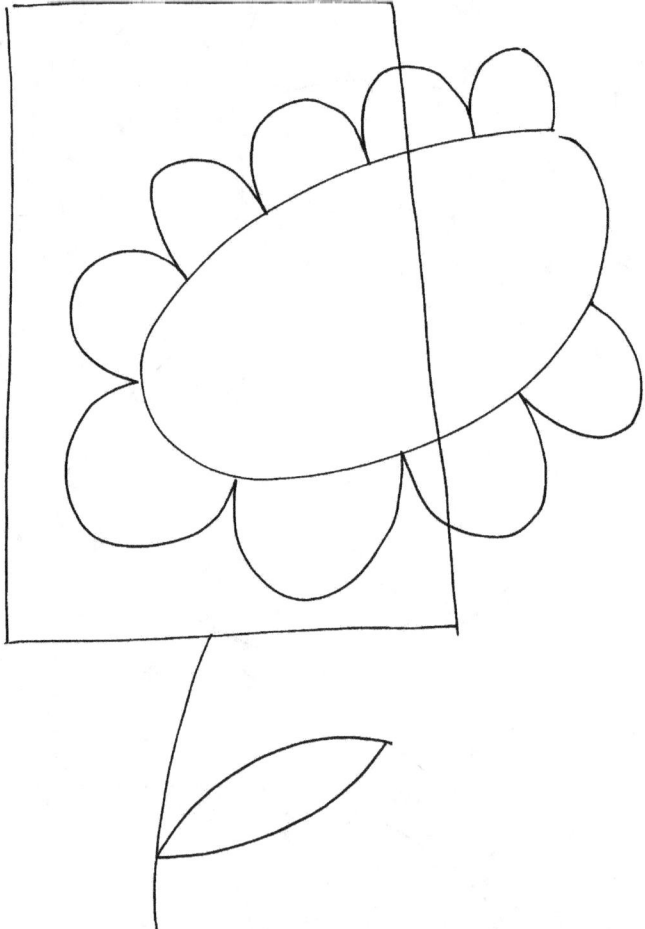

The Flower 4

Create Your NeoWhimsies from the Scratch

*U*se the following pages to create new NeoWhimsies. It could be the imaginative mushrooms and grasshoppers, flowers and birds, umbrellas and hats, anything you like. Draw the flowing line, which creates the sections. Do it with ease. Then, fill the sections that appeared with different repetitive patterns - ornaments. Use the circle, squares, triangles, rectangular, dots, rays, "snakes", small flowers, other objects, their combinations and different variations, different sizes. Some sections leave blank. Use your imagination and artistic intuition. Develop your skills. Draw your NeoWhimsies step-by-step as you learned from this book. When you draw the repetitive patterns, you enter the meditative state of mind, you relax. More you draw, the better your drawings are. Have fun, create, meditate!

Draw your NeoWhimsy here. Create, have fun, meditate!

Draw your NeoWhimsy here. Create, have fun, meditate!

Create Your Repetitive
Patterns Gallery

*U*se the following pages to create repetitive patterns Gallery. Fill each section with different imaginative ornaments - repetitive patterns. Use line, circles, squares, ovals, triangles, zig-zags, rectangular, rays, "snakes", dots, small flowers, other objects. You will use these patterns later in your future NeoWhimsies. Impossible is nothing, use your imagination, develop your skills!

1	2	3
4	5	6
7	8	9

10	11	12
13	14	15
16	17	18
19	20	21

From illustrator Serge E. Mikhailov

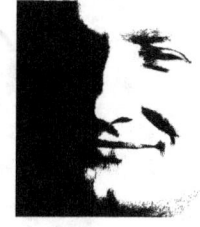

Hello, my name is Serge E. Mikhailov. I like to draw in graphic style! And hope you too! I would like to say thank you to the NeoPopRealism PRESS for cooperation and the new ideas.

I was born in 1970 in Russia, in the City of Khabarovsk, located 19 miles from the Chinese border. In 1998, I began to draw and was influenced by Picasso and Matisse. I authored a book on the self improvement and imagination and now involved in a few Internet projects that help people develop their imagination and the drawing skills (http://hohohu.com).

When I found out about the NeoPopReaism ink drawing style, I thought it is unusual and fun to use the ornamental patterns in the drawing. It was something new to me. The ornament – the patterns – carry the extra emotions and information, the subconscious emotions. This type of drawing is able to hide the inaccuracy and a person can draw without eraser. The NeoPopRealism ink images look complete.

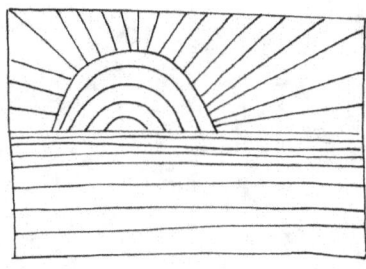

Take a look at a simple picture of the sunset on the left. This drawing is complete and it uses the patterns of NeoPopRealism. Everyone can draw in the NeoPopRealism style!

I ride my bicycle, take photos or draw to relax. When a person draws, he/she uses the sub-consciousness, trying to connect the different concepts in his/her mind. The drawing is a meditative process (trance). If you would like to know what is on your mind, then draw! When you are relaxed, you can draw the wide pictures. When you are full of energy, then you draw the zigzags (ornament). Turn the pictures and you will see the different emotions. If you would like to learn how to draw, I would be happy to teach you!

Conclusion

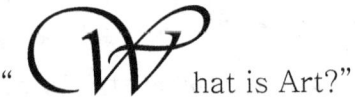

" hat is Art?"

Now, when you learned how to draw the NeoPopRealism ink images – the NeoWhimsies, you might have your answer to this open question. We'd like to hear from you, e-mail us neopoprealismpress@mail.com. Also, if you have a blog, post there the images of your NeoPopRealism ink drawings and a story about how you learned to draw them. And, please, mention there this book with NeoPopRealism creator Nadia Russ. Have a wonderful journey to the world of NeoPopRealism!

NeoPopRealism ten canons for happier life:

1. Be beautiful.

2. Be creative and productive; never stop studying and learning.

3. Be peace-loving, positive-minded.

4. Do not accept totalitarian philosophy.

5. Be free-minded, do the best you can to move the world to peace and harmony.

6. Be family oriented, self-disciplined.

7. Be free spirited. Follow your dreams, if they are not destructive, but constructive.

8. Believe in GOD. God is one. It is harmony and striving for perfection.

9. Be supportive to those who need you, be generous.

10. Create your life as a great adventurous story.

Nadia Russ, 2004

Additional books - teaching / learning material on NeoPopRealism Ink drawing for adults, teenagers and children

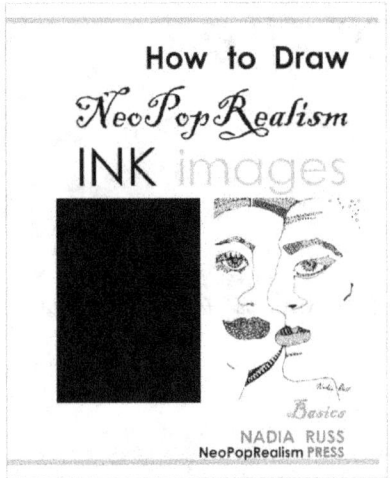

ISBN: 9780615515755
FOR TEENS & ADULTS

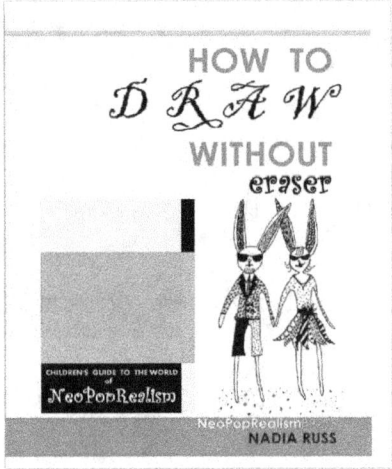

ISBN: 9780615521824
FOR CHILDREN

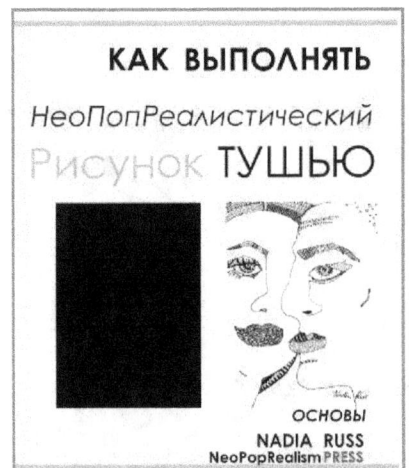

Book "*How to Draw NeoPopRealism Ink Images: Basics*" in Russian translation.
ISBN: 9780615516967

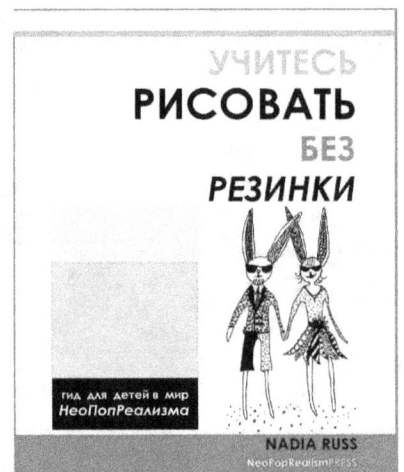

Book "*How to Draw Without Eraser: Backgrounds*" in Russian translation.
ISBN: 9780615523484

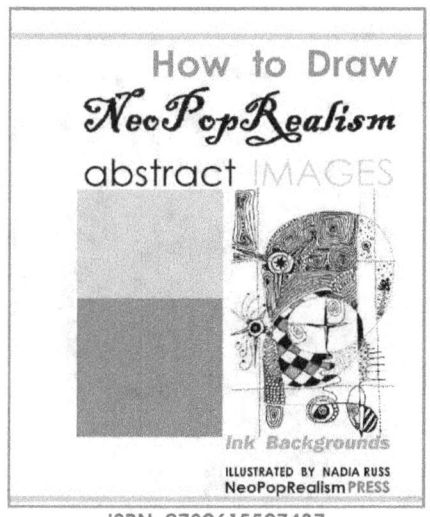

ISBN: 9780615527437
FOR TEENS & ADULTS

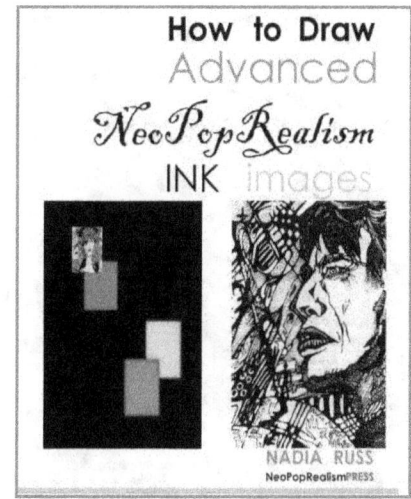

ISBN: 9780615569758
FOR TEENS & ADULTS

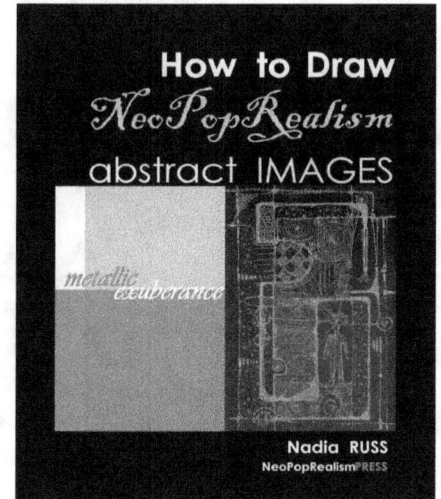

ISBN: 9780615560991
FOR TEENS & ADULTS

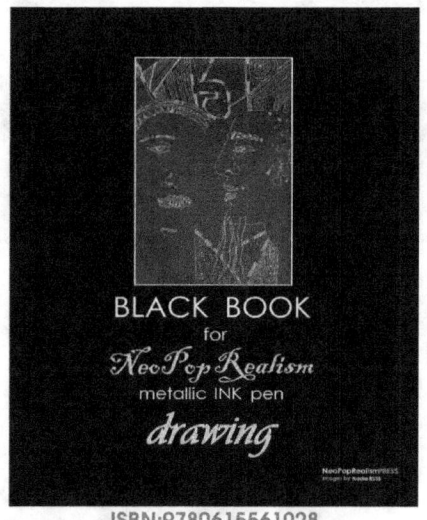

ISBN:9780615561028
FOR ALL AGES & LEVELS

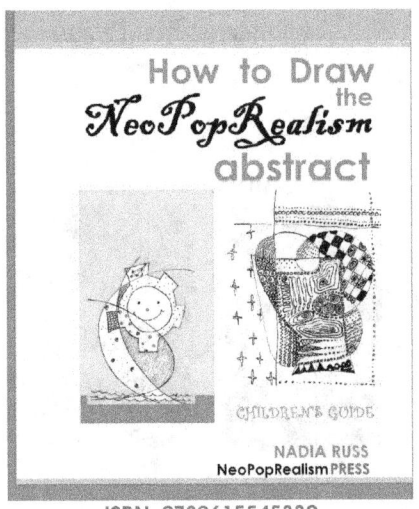

ISBN: 9780615545332

FOR CHILDREN

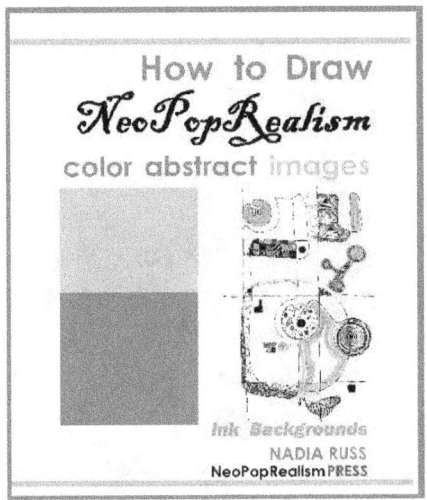

ISBN: 9780615579559

FOR TEENS & ADUTS

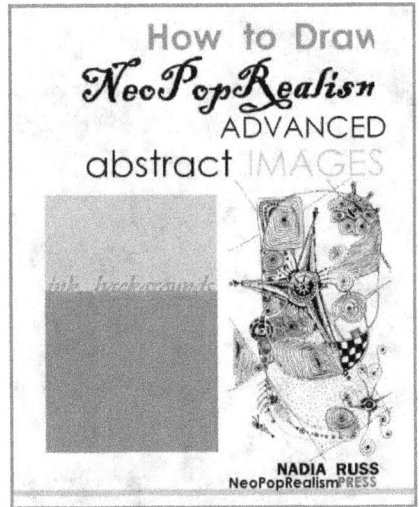

ISBN: 9780615592558

FOR TEENS & ADULTS

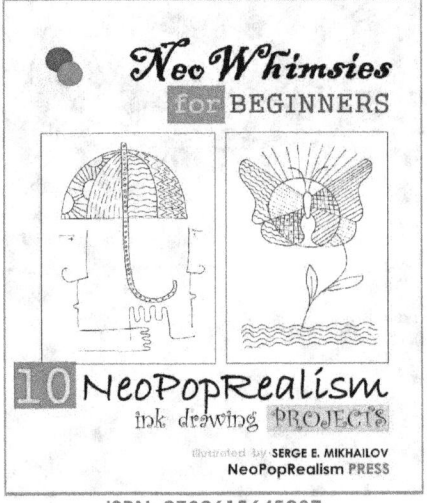

ISBN: 9780615645087

FOR CHILDREN & ARTISANS

www.ingramcontent.com/pod-product-compliance
Lightning Source LLC
Chambersburg PA
CBHW081208180526
45170CB00006B/2259